The process
of
argument

The process of argument

MICHAEL BOYLAN

UNIVERSITY
PRESS OF
AMERICA

Lanham • New York • London

Published in 1993 by
University Press of America®, Inc.
4720 Boston Way
Lanham, Maryland 20706

Originally published in 1988 by Prentice Hall
Copyright © 1988 by Michael Boylan

Library of Congress Cataloging-in-Publication Data
Boylan, Michael.
The process of argument / Michael Boylan.
p.   cm.
Originally published: Englewood Cliffs, N.J. : Prentice Hall, ©1988.
Includes index.
1. English language—Rhetoric.   2. Persuasion (Rhetoric)
3. Language and logic.   4. Reasoning.   I. Title.
[PE1431.B69   1993]   808'.042—dc20   93–12031 CIP

ISBN 0–8191–9065–9 (pbk. : alk. paper)

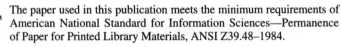
The paper used in this publication meets the minimum requirements of
American National Standard for Information Sciences—Permanence
of Paper for Printed Library Materials, ANSI Z39.48–1984.

For
Arianne and Sean

Contents

Preface

The principal audience for this book is the student of argumentative reasoning. In the past this discipline has been called rhetoric, logic, and English prose composition. Therefore, all these students would be included in the general intention of this work. No particular specialized knowledge about rhetoric, composition, logic, or philosophy is assumed. Everything you need will be found between the covers of this slim volume.

The need for such a primer became evident to me in my teaching. I have taught in both English and in philosophy. When I had classes in composition I found that before I could teach writing, I had to first teach reading. The building block of non-fiction prose is the logical argument. It is upon logical arguments that the entire body of the composition is constructed.

I therefore came to the conclusion that mastery of reading and understanding arguments made possible the reasoned responses to those arguments. I have thus structured this text with these two goals in mind. First, outlining skills are presented. It is here that the tools are made available to confront various types of arguments.

After mastering these skills I move on to constructing reasoned responses to logical arguments. These I call "argument evaluations." The first stage is meant to be a means to the second. I try to show how such a bridge is natural. Having mastered the first step, the student is in a better position to begin the second. Thus the sequential nature of these steps is important.

I would suggest approaching this book according to the given order. However, much of this material is such that students can assimilate it in conjunction with other readings that are being carried on in the course. This is the method I have found successful in my own teaching. First, I present the material briefly, and then I let students follow instructions at their own pace as they integrate these various techniques with whatever subject matter we happen to be studying.

It is in this way that this text can be a useful tool for a variety of classes and purposes. In an introductory composition class one could arrange various essays and use the principles found herein to create logical outlines, and, later, argument evaluations. In an introductory philosophy class or logic class the instructor could continue with normal readings and use this primer as a way to give rigor and structure to the types of responses that students have. So often I hear a student in such a class claim after reading a selection by Descartes or Aristotle, "I know what the author was saying, but I just can't put it into words."

This volume aspires to guide such students. The method proposed can help them not only find words to describe the argument, but to find such words that will exactly recreate the argument. Such a method affords a "way into the work" that otherwise might remain rather opaque to the first-time reader.

Outlining is thus a valuable tool for the academic study of argument required by a study of composition or philosophy. But there are further applications, too. As I mention in the Introduction, the skills of successful argumentation are valuable—perhaps among the most valuable that can be taught in the humanities. This book fills a gap between various handouts that some teachers (myself included) have had to resort to in teaching some of these skills and full logic or composition texts, which have a much more ambitious aim in mind. They aspire to be primary texts for a course, while this modest volume is intended to be a supplement to other readings. The description and exercises have been kept brief, in order to introduce the skill to be mastered and put it into some recognizable context. There is no attempt at being comprehensive. But this is precisely the book's strength. What many students and their professors need and desire is a succinct course of study.

It is with this limited, but practical, purpose in mind that I present this volume with the hope that some of these suggestions will make more accessible the rich world of non-fictional, rhetorical prose.

ACKNOWLEDGMENTS

There are many people who have helped me in the development of this volume in various ways and to differing degrees. To those colleagues and former teachers I am grateful.

My students have also aided my application of this method to the classroom. Their efforts have guided me in my overall scheme.

This book was improved by the publisher's reviewers, and the suggestions of my editor, Joe Heider.

I'd most especially like to note Robert Warburton, Arthur Adkins, and Denis Savage whose advice has led me in profitable directions.

To this list I must also add my wife, Rebecca, whose support and love has sustained me.

Michael Boylan

The process

of

argument

Introduction
understanding and responding to logical argument

Argument—what is it? Does it mean someone is angry with someone else? Is it something to avoid? Many people are unacquainted with argument as the logical means of persuasion.

It is obvious to everyone that the power of persuasion is valuable. In Ancient Greece people spent large sums of money to possess this rare commodity; with it, they felt they could become successful. Other, less mercenary philosophers, such as Plato and Aristotle, extended the study of argument, developing it from an art into a science.

Indeed, today similar attitudes toward persuasion exist. Executive seminars offer training in the art of leadership and positive thinking. These really amount to methods of getting your ideas across to someone else. The motivation for these seminars is success and financial gain.

Likewise, in our universities, the disinterested study of persuasion proceeds under the titles of philosophy, rhetoric, and composition. Both their practical and intellectual exercises have one point in common: They both aspire to construct rules whereby one can properly persuade others.

A full-scale treatment of this topic is beyond the scope of this volume. Instead, this text will act as an initiation that will supplement and enrich various courses of instruction.

Be that as it may, a few things should be noted about the methodology adopted for this present volume and how it intends to aid the student in acquiring the skill of analytic reading and reasoned evaluation.

The first point is that the purpose of argument, *persuasion,* is not a commodity that exists in isolation. One seeks to persuade within a context. This context can be described by the following elements:

Speaker
Audience
Point of Contention
Argument
Common Body of Knowledge

An example of all these elements working together follows:

Sam wants to persuade Kathy to go to the movies. Kathy smiles, but doesn't reply. So Sam lists the great reviews and modestly hints at the advantages of going with him. After all, they're both in the same English Class, love literature, and could have so much to talk about!

In this example the speaker is Sam; the audience is Kathy; the point of contention is "Kathy going to the movie with Sam"; the argument consists of both the movie's quality and the scenario of a good time; the common body of knowledge is their shared aesthetic value system.

The reader is encouraged to identify these elements within the context of arguments he may encounter. Familiarity with these separate roles is useful for acquiring competence in the process of argument.

Several points about argument can be made using the simple structure outlined above. Perhaps the most difficult of these five elements to understand is "the common body of knowledge." This is because this element consists of a collection of facts and shared assumptions about what counts as a proper way to relate facts. These assumptions are a set of logical rules or procedures, and without them, no conclusions can be drawn from the facts. To show some of the difficulties that can occur in even the simplest cases, let us examine the following three examples of common facts:

1. John is six feet tall.
2. It is uncomfortably hot outside today.
3. General Electric is ripe for a corporate takeover.

The above examples differ in several respects. In the first one, presumably, we have an objective fact. But what makes it objective? It is because (1) we have an agreed unit of measurement, and (2) John is set against this standard.

The first statement refers to an agreed standard by which measurements can be made. This is generally unproblematic, but disagreements are possible at this level. For example, someone who opted for the metric system might disagree that measurements should be taken in the English system of weights and measures. (Some awkward cases have arisen over just this issue between the U.S. and the International Track and Field Federation concerning standards of measurement and world records in the high jump and pole vault.)

Conversion tables are available, of course, but the point is that even with very straightforward cases, one must make certain assumptions that, themselves, are not subject to dispute. Without these assumptions, no resolution is possible.

The second statement refers to the use of the measurement standard. Suppose we agree to the English system of weights and measures. Then (2) is about the actual measuring of John against a calibrated yardstick. Again, this seems uncomplicated, but problems can arise. It is possible to set up an agreed standard, and yet disagree about whether the object in question is most appropriately subsumed under it. Such disputes are not uncommon. For example, legal authorities often are at a loss to decide under which statute to try a criminal. Although the law is clear, its application is not.

Thus, even in such straightforward examples as the first common fact above, there are some possible grounds for disagreement. In order to analyze the dispute we need to make exact distinctions which can point to where the disagreement lies. Once this is known, a reasoned response and dialogue are possible.

In the second common fact there is an added factor to be considered: the value judgment of what constitutes "uncomfortably hot." One might agree to a temperature scale and how to read it and still disagree about when to judge a day to be uncomfortably hot. To some this may be seventy-five degrees, while to others it may be ninety degrees. In other words, various theories of what constitutes temperature and how to measure it might be agreed upon, but a value judgment about these facts may also be required. In this case agreement must be reached before the argument may continue.

The first two examples refer to *theory*. Theories contain standards and often sanction judgments connected to these standards.

The third example adds one more level to our model. We may agree about *what* constitutes a corporate takeover and *how* to measure the circumstances (as in the first example); and *when*, in theory, this is a good course of action (the judgment entailed in the second example), but still disagree on whether or not General Electric is in such a position at present. Thus, the judgment necessary to put a theory into practice constitutes the third stage of accepted common facts. This last stage deals in particulars because it is directed toward judgments to act. These judgments cannot be considered apart from real circumstances, because these circumstances, together with the relevant theory, are necessary to determine what is to be done.

All three stages work together sequentially to describe the environmental context of the argument. It is hoped that these brief comments will inspire the reader's appreciation of the importance of this aspect in the process of argument.

The second point is that within the argument itself there are important internal relationships. One of these is the interdependence between the point of contention and the premises. The argument's entire existence—indeed, its reason for being—is solely to put forth the point of contention (called the *conclusion* when it stands in a finished argument). Because of this singular mission, the argument's character must mirror closely that of the point of contention. This creates a mutual dependence between the two so that knowledge of the argument will allow us to know the point of contention, and knowledge of the point of contention will aid us in discovering the argument.

It is true that for any point of contention several arguments may be constructed that will demonstrate that point, but this does not alter the fact that, as stated, the relationship between the two is very close. One way to explain this is that the argument's *premises* and the point of contention mutually imply each other as cause and effect. Such causes have to do with the form or structure of the argument (what the philosopher Aristotle called the "formal cause").

For example, if one wished to make a claim about the best all-time hitter in baseball, one might put forward the following point of contention: "Ted Williams and Rogers Hornsby were the best all-time hitters in baseball." The premises to prove this point cannot have an arbitrary character. They must establish criteria upon which one can judge a hitter to be the best hitter. In this way the *genesis* of the premises is an effect arising from the point of contention.

We began with "Ted Williams and Rogers Hornsby were the best all-time hitters in baseball." In order to be accepted, this point of contention needs sentences that logically support it. These sentences are called *premises*. These premises come to be in order to prove some point of contention (also called a conclusion). Whatever comes to be for the sake of something else, in one sense, can be said to be caused by its originator. The order of genesis refers to the mode through which something comes to be. In this order the point of contention (conclusion) causes the premises.

To set out a simplified example of such an argument we need to establish a standard first. Obviously, as we have seen, setting such standards is controversial. Let us say that the triple-crown leader is the most adequate test of an all-around hitter. The triple crown measures the three primary categories of hitting: batting average, runs batted in, and home runs. Only two players have ever won the triple crown in their leagues more than once: Ted Williams and Rogers Hornsby.

The argument could be set down as displayed in Table One.

Premises 1 through 3 come about from our search to prove point 4 (conclusion). However, seen from the perspective of the finished argument, point 4 is *itself* the effect of premises 1 through 3.* That is, if we

---

* Premises and conclusions are really abstract objects whose truth is independent of what we believe or assent to. However, beliefs and motives are crucial to the way we construct arguments (*order of genesis*), and they provide a useful tool to describe the *order of logical presentation*.

TABLE ONE: Sample Baseball Argument

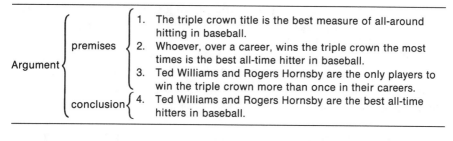

Argument	premises	1.	The triple crown title is the best measure of all-around hitting in baseball.
		2.	Whoever, over a career, wins the triple crown the most times is the best all-time hitter in baseball.
		3.	Ted Williams and Rogers Hornsby are the only players to win the triple crown more than once in their careers.
	conclusion	4.	Ted Williams and Rogers Hornsby are the best all-time hitters in baseball.

assent to premises 1 through 3, we must agree with point 4. The conclusion is the effect of premises 1 through 3 being true.

Thus, in the *order of logical presentation* the conclusion is the effect and the premises are the cause. This arrangement is just the opposite of the *order of genesis*. This relationship is set out in Table Two. The consequence of this is that the premises and the point of contention (conclusion) are seen to be interdependent so that each affects the character of the other. Thus, the argument in Table One, "Ted Williams and Rogers Hornsby are the best all-time hitters in baseball," and the three premises which precede it can influence each other as cause and effect in the manner suggested in Table Two. The direction of this influence depends upon what perspective we take: from the order of genesis or from the order of logical presentation.

When we *construct* our own arguments we are most concerned with the order of genesis. We begin with a statement we're trying to prove and then create premises which will prove it. However, when we are *reading* or *listening* to another's argument, then the order of logical presentation is primary. Keeping these purposes and relationships in mind may help later when we try to engage in each process.

The third point is a caution. Sometimes people try to persuade without employing logical argument. For these individuals, logical argument is supplanted by logical fallacy. The difference between logical argument and logical fallacy is the use of illicit means of persuasion.

Now why would one wish to do this? In the first place, it is often more successful in persuading large numbers of people in a shorter time than logical argument. Thus, if one is selling either advertising time on televi-

TABLE TWO: The Relationship between the Elements of Logical Persuasion

ORDER OF GENESIS	ELEMENTS	ORDER OF LOGICAL PRESENTATION
Effect ↑ Cause	Premises	Cause ↓ Effect
	Conclusion	

sion or space within a magazine, he may receive a quicker return on each dollar by employing logical fallacy rather than logical argument. This need not be the case; advertising *can* pictorially embody logical argument (see exercises in Chapter Four).

The trouble with fallacies is that they depend upon tricks and illusions. They persuade illegitimately. This does not mean that everyone who employs a fallacy could not have constructed a persuasive message using logical argument. In most cases, the use of fallacy merely indicates the rhetorician's preference.

Thus, Acme Widgets may try to persuade the public to purchase their product by placing it between a pair of attractive male and female models attired in evening clothes. The force of the persuasion is the fact that everyone wants to be young, rich, and attractive. The Acme Widget is *associated* with this pleasing picture by the advertiser who wants us to think that we can become young, rich, and attractive by purchasing the Acme Widget.

However, anyone who was pointedly questioned about this connection would surely demur, because no natural, scientific connection can be found between the two. Everyone would agree to this. But still the ads are successful. Why? Because people *do not* consciously question what they are seeing. If they did, they would feel insulted that the Acme Company thinks it can sell its widgets without telling us relevant information such as how its product's features compare with those of its competitors.

It is this unthinking, subliminal reaction that proponents of logical fallacy depend upon. When we fall into their trap, we become slaves to their tricks.

Fortunately, there is a way out. The tool is logic. The power is the mind. One of the beneficial by-products of learning the skills set forth in this book is that you will be less likely to be hoodwinked by such illogical shenanigans. By applying reason properly we acquire a power of self-determination. This free autonomy is inherently desirable—and yet it does not come without some training of our natural mental faculties. This will be discussed further in Chapter Nine.

The fourth point concerns a further incentive for understanding the structure of argument. We all wish, at times, to offer opinions on various questions. Someone sets down an argument such as the one I did on baseball batters. Perhaps you disagree with the argument. What response are you to make? One thing you might say is, "That's all wrong!" or "You're crazy!" But such responses don't convey any specific content other than the fact that, upon hearing the argument, you were put into a negative state of mind.

But unless we can get beyond that point, no discourse is possible. Also, it may be that there is no real disagreement at all, but merely a problem in the way the sentence was expressed.

The tool that allows one to make real progress is *logical analysis.* Analysis literally means "to break up." Therefore, when presented with a composite whole, one must isolate the various parts: speaker, audience, point of contention, argument, and common body of knowledge.

Once analysis has revealed the structure and relationship of these parts, one can look at each part separately and make individual evaluations. It is possible, for example, that one may agree with every premise except one. In this case, all discussion should be focused upon that single point. For if this point can be resolved, then accord is possible. Using our baseball example, such a process might look like the following:

A DIALOGUE BETWEEN SUE AND TOM

TOM: Ted Williams and Rogers Hornsby are the greatest hitters of all time.
SUE: No way.
TOM: It's true.
SUE: How do you figure that?
Tom then provides the argument from Table One.
SUE: Now I see why you think Ted Williams and Rogers Hornsby are so great. But I disagree with your point that whoever wins the triple crown the most times in his career is the best all-time hitter.
TOM: You got a better idea?
SUE: Sure. Home runs. It's obvious. Every fan knows the hardest thing to do is to send the ball over the fence.
TOM: Well, I don't know. If that's true, then Henry Aaron would be the greatest hitter of all time.
SUE: Exactly!

In this dialogue the single point upon which they disagree becomes the topic of discussion. Space does not allow a full investigation of the merits of the point at issue, but it is important that Tom and Sue realize where their disagreement lies: the definition of the best all-time hitter. (The disagreement concerns which measurement standard to use—see our discussion under the first point.)

Finding the crucial point is what analysis is all about. It allows one to see the structure of the argument. Just as scientists search for the critical experiment to prove or disprove their theories, so also the logically minded person searches for critical premises in the argument. Chapters 1 through 3 will set out the rules for such analysis, while Chapters 7 and 8 will discuss the ways to formulate reactions to the arguments once they are set out.

The general principle we're operating under is this: One cannot offer a meaningful and valid opinion on a point of contention unless he or she has first engaged in logical analysis. Otherwise, the reaction will be hopelessly vague and of no value.

For example, if someone asks you how you liked a movie and you reply "It was good" or "It stunk," you are giving very little meaningful information. Perhaps your measurement standard for judging movies depends upon how many characters are killed in the plot: More than ten killings rates a positive response; less than ten a negative one. Obviously, then, without knowing the measurement scale and the value judgments made from that scale, any response given is almost meaningless.

In these brief remarks I have touched upon some of the basic features of logical argument and why it is of such importance to become competent at it. Throughout our lives we are constantly bombarded with points of contention: whether it is an agreement to buy a car, negotiating a raise, responding to a business memo, writing a letter to the editor, or just being an articulate, autonomous human being. There is power in understanding the rules and structure of argument. This potent capacity has been recognized since the time of the Ancient Greeks. They sacrificed greatly to gain these mysterious gifts because they believed them to be of enduring and inherent value.

These pages seek to initiate the reader into an acquaintance with this power.

READING QUESTIONS

Answers for selected exercises are given at the end of the book.

1. What are the elements that make up the context of argument?
2. Give an example of all these elements working together.
3. Name at least two of the three ways by which common facts may be disputed.
4. How do the orders of *genesis* and *logical presentation* differ?
5. Why do people employ logical fallacies?
6. How should one confront logical fallacy?

CHAPTER ONE

What is an outline?

TOPICAL VS. LOGICAL

The method of logical analysis taught in this volume is that of *logical outlining*. A logical outline is different from the style of outline most of us were taught: a *topical outline*. The topical outline provides a summary of all that occurs within a given passage. It is a condensed presentation that allows one to skim over the high points of a given work.

In contrast to a topical outline, the logical outline seeks only to present arguments and points of contention. Any other material, such as classificatory remarks and various enumerations, is omitted from the logical outline.

For example, consider the contrasting outlines that can be constructed from the following passage:

> What sort of person makes the best high-level manager? We all know that many kinds of people enter management. They range across the spectrum of human nature—from the timid, sniveling and spineless, to the aggressive high-powered motivators. But surely we all know that the future of our companies depends upon the quality of upper-level management. Therefore, it is apropos to ask what quality is inherent in the best of these leaders of industry. In three words, it is a "calculated risk taker." This can easily be seen from the fact that initiating bold, new action, which is a top-level manager's job, involves taking risks. The policies of the past have to be reexamined and, if found wanting, then bold, new, risky paths must be explored.
>
> Obviously, though, one cannot go off willy nilly. Some savvy and calculation are required since these risk takers are more often than not the winners at the end of the day. This is what has made American industry great, and it must continue if we are to remain strong.

LOGICAL OUTLINE

1. A high-level manager must be able to boldly lead a company away from policies of the past. (*assertion*)
2. To move away from policies of the past is to take a new direction. (*fact*)
3. Initiating bold new directions involves taking risks. (*fact*)
4. High-level managers must be risk takers. (*1–3*)
5. Calculated risk taking is more successful than uncalculated risk taking. (*fact*)
6. High-level managers must employ the most successful strategies open to them. (*assertion*)
7. High-level managers must be calculated risk takers. (*4, 5, 6*)

TOPICAL OUTLINE

I. Types of Managers
  A. Timid
    1. Sniveling
    2. Spineless
  B. Aggressive
    1. High-powered
    2. Motivator
  C. Similar to cross-sections of humanity
II. Future of Industry
  A. Lies with upper-level managers
  B. Quality managers make good companies
    1. Risk takers
    2. Bold new action
    3. Re-examine policies of past
    4. Tempered with savvy and calculation
III. Past Success of American Industry
  A. Depends upon risk-taking managers
  B. Must continue for the future

Let us consider, in reverse order, some of the differences between the topical and logical outline and then highlight the strengths of each.

The topical outline can give you a summary of what is contained within a book or lecture. By condensing the material, through the use of key words and phrases, the reader can recall the flow and order of the text. Such an outline might be useful for creating an encapsulated reconstruction, or for boning up on a large amount of material at a glance. It is for this latter purpose that topical outlining is usually taught in grammar school.

The logical outline, in contrast, is not a summary. It is an exact reconstruction of the argument contained within a given passage. Some textual material is omitted. There is *no classification* found in logical outlines unless it is directly relevant to the argument at hand. Thus, in the above example, the classification into the two types of managers is not included.

Also omitted are various side remarks. In the above example the depictions of "sniveling," "spineless," "high-powered," and "motivator" are all side comments. The remarks on the future of American industry are also side comments, since these remarks are not accompanied by an appropriate argument.

What remains is an exact depiction of the internal structure of the sentences meant logically to persuade us to accept some point of contention. This outline admittedly misses certain parts of a passage; thus, it is not comprehensive. But it is a more detailed and useful tool for understanding an argument than the topical outline. If one wanted to formulate an objection to this argument, the topical outline would not afford the reader the same view of all the logical relationships between sentences that the logical argument does.

For this reason the logical outline can be viewed as a specialized form of outlining. It has a precise mission. But if one wishes to be comprehensive in note taking, then this form could be supplemented with a topical outline.

THE PURPOSE OF AN OUTLINE

However, inasmuch as most books and articles seek to be persuasive rather than merely descriptive, the logical outline becomes the single most important form of reaction. It forces one to come to grips with exactly what is being said.

We have all heard people say, "I know what the author is saying, it's just that I can't form an outline of it." This statement is misleading. What the speaker means is that he or she has a general, vague idea of what is going on in the passage. It is for this reason that an outline cannot be formed, since logical outlining requires more precision than he or she currently possesses. The speaker's comment can be illustrated by Table Three. When the speaker claims an understanding of the text but is unable to outline it, he or she is really saying that more than C% but less than A% is understood. However, it is the contention of this book that unless one has acquired a mastery of a text of at least A%, a sufficient level of competence has not been met. Therefore, one advantage of logical outlining is that it demands a higher level of excellence from the reader.

It has been my experience in the classroom that most students are searching for opportunities to work in depth and really master the material. Often, in an effort to be comprehensive and broad in scope, the student is burdened with so many pages of reading that all he or she can hope to achieve is C%. This breeds not only frustration but an entire framework of mediocrity. There is a very limited benefit if most of one's courses require a surface, facile level of comprehension in exchange for large, survey quantities of processed material.

TABLE THREE: Degrees of a Logical Argument's Comprehension

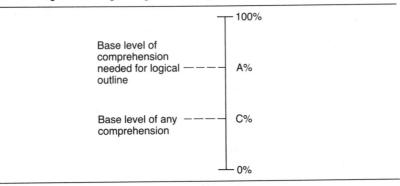

At the very least, people should be given the opportunity to work in a depth that encourages multiple readings and slow, painstaking interaction with the text. I suggest that in the beginning, you ask your instructor to flag the most important arguments *after* you have read them once. This will provide some further structure from which to create your outlines. As the course progresses, you will develop toward identifying the arguments yourself and creating your own reconstruction from these judgments. It is at this final stage that you can justifiably feel that you are getting the most out of the argumentative prose.

FAIRNESS IN RECONSTRUCTION

One final word must be made on fairness in reconstructing arguments. Often when encountering a logical argument one is faced with what seems to be a very simple-minded mistake or superficial flaw. One response to this discovery is to pounce on it and use it to reject the entire argument. However, I think such an approach is not useful. This is because the author need merely make a slight alteration concerning the supposed flaw and the argument will be saved.

It is better to note the alleged error and then make the alteration yourself. In this way you are operating on the principle that you desire to evaluate the strongest version of the argument. Finding superficially weak interpretations is like finding "straw men" who are easy targets. It proves very little when one defeats a straw man. It is better to give the author every benefit of the doubt and view the case in the best possible light. We can state this principle of fairness as follows:

> Always reconstruct an argument in its strongest form even if it requires correcting trivial errors (though these may be noted elsewhere).

An example of this might be derived from our earlier sample on the qualities of the high-level manager. Now it is possible that one might read this passage and find the following points to disagree with:

1. There are no timid, spineless managers.
2. Risk evaluation is a much more complicated field than the passage suggests.
3. More traits are needed in a successful manager than simply calculating risk taking.

Many more things could be said, of course, but these three reactions typify a large group of possible responses. Point 1 may be true, but what effect does an incorrect classification have on the argument's point of contention? None. This point can easily be conceded without weakening the argument at all. Therefore, under the principle of fairness outlined above, it would not be an appropriate avenue for evaluation.

Point 2 may also be correct, but unless one could show that the simplification engaged in distorts the force of the normative background condition of which it is a part, then it will have no significant impact upon the conclusion.

The distinction in point 2 may be one of degrees. If this is the case the student may feel some alteration of the premise is necessary. Under the principle of fairness the student is obliged to do so after duly observing in a note that such a change is required to make the argument valid.

Finally in point 3 we have a statement that does indeed affect the conclusion. If calculated risk taking was intended as a sufficient condition for high-level management, then we would only have to go down to the horse track to hire the next batch of senior-level officials. Rather, the student must make the charitable assumption that the author intends to highlight *necessary* rather than *sufficient* conditions.

By illustrating a necessary condition, the rhetorician only needs to show that the manager must have this particular trait. It says nothing about what else might be needed. To attack the writer because sufficient conditions have not been offered as well would be to require the writer to provide material beyond the purpose of the writing. This is surely unfair—unless you also wish to attack that purpose itself.

The reader of goodwill approaches a passage and decides that something important is missing. But then it must be judged whether the alleged error is one which is: (a) really important to the conclusion, and (b) cannot be rectified by relatively minor means (such as assuming a necessary rather than a sufficient condition).

Such restrictions are important to observe both out of fairness to the writer involved and in order to save one's attention for those parts of the argument that are essential to the view being put forth. For it is really this essential point of view that lies at the heart of the argument. Finding and zeroing in on it provides a much more productive use of one's efforts.

READING QUESTIONS

1. What is a topical outline?
2. What is a logical outline?
3. When is it appropriate to use a logical outline and when a topical outline?
4. How does logical outlining affect reading comprehension?
5. What is the "principle of fairness"? Why do we need it?

CHAPTER TWO

Mechanics of outlining

This chapter will provide the basic tools for logical outlining. Both the orders of logical presentation and genesis will be discussed. In addition, an appendix of specialized interests is included at the end of the chapter.

The student is encouraged to read the following example closely and then to refer to it while reading the rest of the chapter.

EDITORIAL IN THE *HOMETOWN GAZETTE*

Residents of fair Hometown, we've got a problem—a big problem. This problem must be addressed now! What I am talking about are *potholes!* Yes, you have seen them arise and grow each spring when the winter thaw leaves its debris behind. At first they were only fissures, but now they threaten road safety and the general condition of our automobiles. Do you know what can happen to your car when you hit one of those potholes at 40 miles per hour? Your axle gets bent out of shape. And axles are expensive to replace.

It's therefore time for a change! The city needs to fix its potholes. Oh, I know the mayor says there is no room in the city budget for any more cost cutting in order to fix potholes. And he's right. The budget is tight as a drum. Therefore we must raise taxes to pay for the repairs; we can't delay. Write His Honor today. The city needs to raise taxes to fix those potholes!

LOGICAL OUTLINE

1. [The city's residents prize their automobiles' general condition and their own safety. (*fact*)]
2. There are many large potholes in the city. (*fact*)
3. Large potholes harm the condition of automobile axles as well as general driving safety. (*fact*)
4. The city needs to fill its potholes. (*1–3*)
5. The city is presently operating with a budget that cannot be trimmed. (*assertion*)

6. [Filling potholes costs money. (*fact*)]
7. [The only way a city can find money for a project is by cutting spending or by raising taxes. (*assertion*)]
8. The city can fix potholes only by raising taxes. (*5–7*)

9. The city needs to raise taxes to fix potholes. (*4, 8*)

VOCABULARY

(For other terms see also the glossary at the end of the book.)

Dividing the text.   The text may be divided into three parts: argument, classification, and side comments.

Proposition.   A declarative sentence with truth value.

Premise.   These are the building blocks of argument. The individual sentences of an argument are called premises. In the sample above, the sentences numbered 1 through 8 are all premises. Collectively, the premises cause one to accept the point of contention; they logically imply the conclusion.

Conclusion.   The point of contention. It is what the argument aims for. In the sample, item 9 is the conclusion. The justification of a conclusion is always an inference. A line (such as that under item 8) or three dots—∴—is used in logical outlines to set off the conclusion.

Argument.   An argument consists of at least two sentences, one of which logically follows from the other. The statement said to follow is the conclusion and the supporting statement is the premise. The vehicle which allows one to move from premise to conclusion is called an inference.

In this book we will present arguments that generally consist of at least two premises as these are the most common arguments. Therefore, the rules of argument put forth in this chapter will primarily be directed at these arguments.

There are two broad classes of argument: inductive and deductive. Chapter Two will concentrate on deductive argument while inductive argument will be presented in Chapter Three.

Classification.   One of the three divisions of the text. This is a mode of analysis in which classes are created on the basis of a division made in the common body of knowledge (see Introduction).

Side comments.   One of the three divisions of the text. Anything which is not an argument or a classification will be labeled a side comment. This label does not imply that these comments are of no value. However, they are not the primary focus of this book.

Justification.   A justification comes after a premise and is the proximate reason for accepting the premise. Three kinds of justification are used to aid in creating an evaluation. They have been divided in this way for their utility in constructing essays. The three types of justification are: assertion, fact, and inference.

Assertion—This is the weakest justification. It means that the premise is true simply because one person has said it. The truth content of the proposition involved may be doubted. In the above sample, premises 5 and 7 are supported by 'assertion.'

Fact—This is the second-strongest justification. It means that most listeners would accept the given truth put forth as objectively correct. When outlining historical texts one should make reference to the beliefs of the time, such as "the earth is the center of the universe," which might count as fact for speakers before the seventeenth century. In the above sample, premises 1, 2, 3, and 6 are justified as 'fact.'

Inference—This is formally the strongest justification. It will generally consist of at least two premises. (In some special cases one premise might count as an inferential justification in a deductive argument. This is called an immediate inference. Also, if you find that you have *more* than four premises listed as a justification—check your work! Chances are that you have compressed two inferences that should remain separate.)

The force of the inference arises from the combination of premises with our common sense. For example, if one accepts premises 1 through 3 in the sample, then he must also accept premise 4. Thus the justification for accepting premise 4 is simply our having accepted premises 1 through 3. When this connection is such that it cannot be doubted, the inference is called *tight*. When one can still doubt the inference, it is called *loose*. For example, in the following argument—(a) dropping a water balloon from the second story window causes the passerby to become wet; but (b) a water balloon was not dropped; therefore, (c) the passerby did not get wet (a,b)—the inference at (c) is loose because it can be doubted.* It is possible the passerby got wet via another means, such as a rainstorm; thus, the inference at (c) is loose and unacceptable.

Suppressed premise. (See also Chapter Five.) These are premises that are needed to make an inference but are not explicitly made by the writer. In the sample, premises 1, 6, and 7 are suppressed. To show their special status these premises are placed within brackets.

One important caution: When adding new premises be sure the added material is in the spirit of the author's other positions; you would not want to add something that the original author would not have supported.

Interlocking premises. Interlocking premises refer to a property of an argument that obtains when all the premises are represented directly or indirectly in the conclusion's inference. In the sample there are eight premises. Premises 4 and 8 are found directly in the conclusion. Premises 1, 2, and 3 are found in premise 4. Since premise 4 is directly in the conclusion, 1, 2, and 3 are indirectly in the conclusion. Likewise, premises 5, 6, and 7 are found in 8, so that premises 5, 6, and 7 are also indirectly in the conclusion. Thus, in the sample all the premises are found directly or indirectly in the conclusion. This means that the sample argument possesses interlocking premises.

Valid argument. An argument is valid when all the inferences are tight and all the premises are interlocking. In a valid argument if one were to accept all the premises, he would *have* to accept the conclusion. Be careful to observe that nothing is said here about the truth of the premises themselves. All that is asserted is that *if* we accept the premises, we must accept the conclusion. Thus, this argument—(a) all cats drink beer; and (b) all beer drinkers are good bowlers; ∴ (c) all cats are good bowlers—is valid, though both its premises are false. But if we accept them we must accept the conclusion. Thus we can see that validity is strictly a formal relationship between premises and conclusion. Understanding validity in this way will help with writing evaluations.

Sound argument. An argument is sound if it is valid and all its premises are true. Thus in the example above about cats and bowling, though it is valid, it is unsound. When an argument is sound, we must accept the conclusion.

Chain argument (also called sorites). A chain argument occurs when the conclusion of one argument becomes a premise in a later argument. If we assume interlocking premises, then the truth of the chain argument depends upon the truth of all its constituents. The arguments thus become interdependent; their fates are tied together. Often sorites consist of a number of these arguments built into a long chain, all dependent upon each other. The whole is only as strong as its weakest link.

RULES

THE ORDER OF LOGICAL PRESENTATION
RULES FOR ASSESSING ANOTHER'S
ARGUMENT

I. Finding the argument and outlining it.
   A. Preliminary reading.
      1. First reading. Define a section of text, such as a chapter, and read it rapidly. Don't stop. Don't take notes. Just read. Go quickly; almost skimming. After this reading mark down the key points you remember.
      2. Second reading. With your sketchy first reading notes in front of you go through the text again. This time take a pencil and make a

* Note: a separate set of rules exists for checking inductive arguments: See Chapter 3.

check in the margin each time you feel an important point is being made. Read in your book at a normal pace. After you finish, go back and decide whether any of your checks can be combined with any others. Divide your text into sections according to these notations.

  B. Outlining.
      1. Titling and labeling. Take each section of text you have demarcated above and assign a title to that section. This title should reflect the point of the passage. Next to your title indicate whether this section of text is an argument, classification, or side comment.
      2. Argument reconstruction. Take all the sections that are arguments and compare titles. Combine any sections that are essentially identical. Then take one of the titles and concentrate on that portion of text. Your title will become the conclusion of the argument.

Next, determine what material in that passage might be used to logically support the conclusion. List these points. Put each statement into the form of a succinct proposition using your own words. Now set your text aside and try to combine the various propositions into inferences that eventually will cause your conclusion. You may have to add premises of your own creation in order to do this. Remember, all premises are to be in your own words. Bracket all suppressed premises (the ones you add).
      3. Test the argument for validity and soundness.

II. Testing for validity.
  A. Interlocking premises. Determine whether the proper argument has interlocking premises. If not, alter the argument so that it has interlocking premises (adding suppressed premises when necessary). To determine whether an argument has interlocking premises, (step one) begin with the conclusion and note which premises are directly present in the justification. Next (step two), note which other premises are associated directly with those already noted as being in the conclusion. Follow this procedure again until all direct relationships are accounted for. Finally (step three), make a list of all premises noted and compare this list to the numbers of premises. If they are identical, then there are interlocking premises. From the sample: step one shows that premises 4 and 8 are the justification of the conclusion. Step two shows that premises 1, 2, and 3 are directly in premise 4; and premises 5, 6, and 7 are directly in 8. Step three shows that the sum of direct and indirect premises tied to conclusion 1, 2, 3, 4, 5, 6, 7, 8 is equal to the premises of argument 1, 2, 3, 4, 5, 6, 7, 8 ∴ the sample argument has interlocking premises.
  B. Tight inferences. Determine whether the argument has tight inferences. If not, alter the argument so that the inferences are tight (adding suppressed premises when necessary). To determine whether the argument has tight inferences, begin with the inference in the conclusion. Read the two to four premises used in the inferential justification. Then read the conclusion itself. Does the conclusion follow from those premises exactly? You may have to try this several times before you are sure. Think critically: Is there any way you could accept those premises and *deny* the conclusion?* If there is, then the concluding inference is loose and must be corrected.

Next, repeat this procedure for each of the inferences found among the premises. In each case the inference must be tight. If you

---

* This does not apply to inductive arguments. See Chapter 3.

engage in any corrections the entire process should be repeated lest your correction of one premise involves the weakening of another inference. For example, in the sample, first one would read premises 4 and 8 and then determine whether the conclusion must be accepted. Finding the answer positive, premises 5, 6, and 7 would be read to determine whether premise 8 must be accepted. Finally, premises 1, 2, and 3 are read with premise 4. After going through this process one can deduce that the inferences are tight.

    C. Judgment of validity. After the premises have been found to be interlocking and tight, one may judge the argument valid.

III. Testing for soundness. After judging an argument to be valid, then examine:

    A. Truth of premises—Assertions. Begin your investigation of the truth of the premises by examining those premises whose justification is an assertion. Since the assertion is the weakest form of justification, it is most probable that any disagreements will occur here. When you find a disagreement, list the general points you have against it in order to help you write an evaluation (see Chapters Seven and Eight).

    B. Truth of premises—Facts. After surveying the assertions, determine whether you would wish to challenge any of the facts as being incorrect. Caution must be used when evaluating historical arguments. One cannot generally blame an historical audience for having accepted some scientific truism (such as the earth being the center of the universe). Any evaluation of an argument made by an historical figure should be charitable with respect to the "best available evidence."

    C. Truth of premises—Inferences. Since these have been checked for validity, no investigation is needed here.

    D. Judgment of soundness. After completing steps one and two, one can conclude that all the premises are true. If they are, then since you've already judged it to be valid, the argument is sound.

IV. Testing for accuracy. After having set out the argument and tested it for validity and soundness, it is wise to return to the passage outlined. Have you captured the intention of the text? Are all additions to the argument in accord with the author's overall viewpoint? Has your wording of the premises been faithful to the meaning that the author intended? If the answer to any of these questions is 'no' then you must return to the passage and make your corrections. Afterwards repeat points II, III, and IV.

V. Assessment of the argument. If the argument is judged to be valid, sound, and accurate, then the conclusion is termed "true" and must be accepted. If it is found wanting in validity, then decide whether this can be rectified by some small change. The principle of fairness dictates that you make any changes that can save an argument's validity so long as: (a) The change is not contrary to another position taken by the author; and (b) you duly note that you have made such a change to save the argument.

    After completing steps I through V, you are now prepared to begin an evaluation.

THE ORDER OF LOGICAL GENESIS
RULES FOR CREATING YOUR OWN
ARGUMENTS

I. Begin with the conclusion. Find out what you want to say. Your thoughts may be fuzzy. To aid in clarifying them set down a thesis statement in the form of a succinct proposition.

II. Creating a supporting argument. This consists of the following four steps:
   A. Listing and titling. Make a list of all the reasons you believe support your thesis. When the list is complete try to combine your various sentences into groups. Then assign a title to each group. The title should be in the form of a proposition.
   B. Inferential combinations. Next, formulate the other sentences in the group into propositions as well. At any point you may add or subtract further sentences. Finally, arrange your titles so that some kind of inferential arrangement exists between them. Remember, your overall goal is to prove your thesis.
   C. Finalizing the argument. Add or subtract various premises in order to formulate your argument. Keep in mind the rules for assessing the argument. The object here is to fine tune your effort so that it conforms to the logical rules.
   D. Assessment. Assess your argument according to the manner prescribed in the order of logical presentation. When you find an error, correct and reassess the whole.

III. The final product. Congratulations, you have created a logical argument which may be used as a guide for constructing an entire essay. Each of the inferences in your supporting argument can count as a paragraph. The inference itself is the topic sentence for that paragraph. The supporting sentences in the inference become the body of the paragraph. Of course, an outline is the bare skeleton for your prose essay. Other sentences will be needed to create a smooth effect. These other elements might include classification for clarity and side comments that will expand and develop the point you are trying to get across.

APPENDIX: INDIRECT ARGUMENT

A special category of argument should be mentioned in this chapter: the indirect argument. This form of argument varies from the stated form in one major way: Instead of having the point of contention proved positively, the logical complement is disproved, or the possible choices are narrowed to one. Thus, indirect argument works in two ways: (a) through logical complements (*reductio ad absurdum*), or (b) through the principle of remainders.

Logical Complements (*reductio ad absurdum*)

This type of argument works on a very simple principle: If we want to prove a point, we first assume its opposite and then show how that opposite leads us into an absurd (false) state of affairs. Since the opposite leads to an obvious falsity, the original point must be correct.

EXAMPLE

"Very good, Cephalus," I said. "But what is the definition of Justice? Is it to tell the truth and to pay your debts? No more? And is this definition even correct?

"Suppose a friend deposits his weapons with me. When he did this he was perfectly in control. Later, when he is mad he asks for them back. Should I give them to him? Nobody would sanction this or call such an action right anymore than they would require me to always speak the truth to my mad friend."

"This is true," he said.

"But then we were not right to say that Justice is telling the truth and repaying that which had been previously given."

Plato, *Republic* I 331^{c}1−^{d}3*

Thesis: Justice ≠ speaking the truth and paying one's debts.

Assume Antithesis: Justice = speaking the truth and paying one's debts.

Antithesis leads to Absurdity: One should provide a madman with weapons.

∴Therefore, antithesis is wrong and thesis is proven.

Comment: Notice that this method relies on there being two and only two logical states, true and false, and that if an antithesis is shown to be absurd (false), then its opposite, the thesis, must be true. This relationship between sentences is called contradictory opposites.

It is important to sharpen one's understanding of opposites since this relationship is crucial for the operation of *reductio ad absurdum*.

THE FOUR PROPOSITIONS

"All swans are white" means "Everything that is a swan is also white."

"No swans are white" means "Nothing that is a swan is also white."

"Some swans are white" means "There is at least one swan which is white."

"Some swans are not white" means "There is at least one swan which is not white."

These may be combined as shown in Table Four where the sentences marked A and O and those marked E and I are contradictory opposites. These are the only relationships from which, in every case, one can immediately deduce the truth value of one statement from that of another.

In Example One the *thesis* could be rewritten as an 'O' statement: "Some cases of telling the truth and paying one's debts *are not* cases of Justice." The corresponding *antithesis* could be written as an 'A' statement: "All cases of telling the truth and paying one's debts are cases of Justice."

By showing the latter is false we *have* shown the former to be true.

Caution on reductio *arguments.*   The major caution here is that one is actually dealing in contradictory opposites. These are sentences whose complements have opposite truth values. However, there is another brand of opposites called *contrary* or *polar* opposites which have a different logical relation.

* All translations are by the author.

TABLE FOUR: Contradictory Opposites

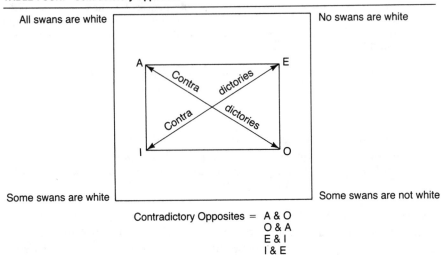

Contradictory Opposites = A & O
O & A
E & I
I & E

Contrary opposites may both be false. In other words, proving one false does not entail the other is true. For example, take these two sentences: "All the sales associates in Johnson's Realty are in the Million-Dollar Club," and "None of the sales associates in Johnson's Realty are in the Million-Dollar Club." If only one third of the sales associates in this company are actually in the Million-Dollar Club, then both the above propositions are false. Thus, proving one to be false does not entail the other being true. We can, therefore, conclude that 'A' and 'E' statements are not contradictory opposites since both may be false. Instead, they are called contrary opposites.

Likewise, if we compare an 'I' and 'O' proposition (see Table Four) we have: "Some of the sales associates in Johnson's Realty are in the Million-Dollar Club" and "Some of the sales associates in Johnson's Realty are not in the Million-Dollar Club." Proving one of these statements true does not prove the other false. They may both be true if at least one member (but not all) of Johnson's Realty is a member of the Million-Dollar Club.

We can therefore conclude that 'I' and 'O' statements are not contradictory opposites since both may be true. Instead, these are called subcontrary opposites.

Reductio ad absurdum only works when the thesis and antithesis are related as contradictory opposites. When this relationship exists, indirect argument by logical complements can be a powerful tool of persuasion.

CHAPTER THREE

Induction

There are two large classifications of argument: deductive and inductive. This chapter will sketch out the difference and illustrate some of the special problems involved in outlining inductive arguments.

EXAMPLE ONE

A. All people are mortal.
    Sally is a person.

    Sally is mortal.
B. Every person on historical record has died within 200 years of their birth.
    Sally is a person.

    Sally is mortal.

Comment: The difference between the above arguments is the manner by which the conclusion follows from the premises. In example A the conclusion follows *necessarily*. If the premises are true (and the inferences valid), the conclusion will also be true.

In example B the conclusion follows *contingently*. It is still possible for the conclusion to be false even if the premises are true.

Two things can be said about this difference: (a) Deductive inference makes explicit mediate relationships already present; and (b) inductive inference goes *beyond* that which is present and points to something *new*. This something new is either a *generalization* or a *causal relationship*.

These two points will be the focus of this chapter. It may be set out as follows:

Generalization
   Enumeration
   Analogy
Causation
   Mill's Method

GENERALIZATION

Enumeration and analogy are two of the most common methods by which generalizations may be formed. When employed correctly they are indispensable tools for inquiry. When utilized improperly they lead us into error.

In proper generalization broad statements are created from a sample that is comprehensive. This means that it is large and varied enough to generate the general conclusion. In addition, the practitioner must be a dispassionate observer so as not to bias the findings.

Jointly, these three conditions help insure proper results. Throughout this discussion on induction pay careful attention to the place of the common body of knowledge. Often, it is the status of these background conditions that can make the difference between a good and bad argument (see also Chapter Nine on Logical Fallacy).

Enumeration

In enumerative induction the strategy is first to list all the observed properties of something with the objective of making a generalization about that type of thing. Then, one draws a conclusion about all members of the class from premises that are about the observed members.

EXAMPLE TWO

After listing all the physical traits of thirty people who successfully survived the malaria outbreak, it was found that all of them had sickle-shaped red blood cells.

∴ All people with sickle-shaped red blood cells will be more successful in surviving exposure to malaria.

OUTLINE

1. A comprehensive list of physical traits made of thirty people after an outbreak of malaria showed that these people shared the common characteristic of having sickle-shaped red blood cells. (*fact*)

2. These thirty people were the survivors among a larger group exposed to malaria. (*fact*)

3. Anyone with sickle-shaped red blood cells will be more successful in surviving exposure to malaria. (*1, 2*)

Comment: Enumeration is one device that enables one to create generalizations. However, it is clear that problems can occur. If the evidence presented in the examination is not exhaustive, or if the case under examination is atypical, then one is liable to make a mistake (see the fallacy of incomplete evidence). For example, it might be true that most of the Nobel Prize winners of the 1980s were European or American, but that does not make Bishop Tutu of South Africa into a European or an American.

Though enumerative induction is imperfect we can try to minimize our chances of error by making sure the sample is sufficiently large and varied, and that the researcher is unbiased. By keeping these conditions in mind, we increase our odds for success.

Analogy

This is a common and productive form of inductive reasoning. Analogy rests on the assumption that objects that are similar in certain respects will also be similar in other respects as well.

EXAMPLE THREE

1. When rats are fed food that has been seasoned with large amounts of salt, they die much sooner than the control group. (*fact*)
2. Humans and rats have certain physiological similarities. (*fact*)
3. Salt must lower the life expectancy in humans, too. (*1, 2*)

Comment: The move from rats to humans is based upon an assumption that both species have digestive similarities which make experiments on one species apply to the other as well. This means that the similarities focused upon in the example are relevant. The presence of this common physiological system increases the chances that the effect experienced by one will also be experienced by the other.

This is where one must be careful. Obviously, there are instances in which the similarity is not relevant and there is no connection between the common trait and the new generalization which is sought. The two may be somewhat independent. For example, Joe may have won the raffle twice while wearing his red flannel shirt. This does not mean that wearing the red flannel shirt a third time has anything to do with winning the raffle a third time. The analogy is improper.

In order for analogy to be effective there must be some connection between the two traits such that the possession of the first increases the probability of the second. This increase must, itself, be the consequence of some mechanism (at least in principle).

To understand whether such mechanisms exist requires reference to the common body of knowledge (see Introduction). This enables us to see how the generalization created in the conclusion fits with other information we already possess. For example, if the new conclusion is in contradiction with, or is inconsistent with, the common body of knowledge, then one might have some doubt about the generalization. If it *is* correct, then we will need more than just a generalization to back us up. This further support will come from the concept of Causation.

CAUSATION

Within our common body of knowledge there are a great many causal connections which we make via this form of induction. These come about through an intricate mental mechanism that includes our memories of certain occurrences which are constantly conjoined to others. This can work from cause to effect or from effect to cause.

EXAMPLE FOUR

A. 1. The clouds are darkening. (*fact*)
    2. The wind is picking up. (*fact*)
    3. There's a funny sensation in the air. (*fact*)
    4. It is going to rain. (*1, 3*)

B. 1. The ground is soggy. (*fact*)
    2. There are pools of water everywhere. (*fact*)
    3. It must have rained. (*1, 2*)

Comment: In example A we are presented with circumstances which generally indicate that it is going to rain. This is an inference from cause to effect. The argument makes a *prediction* about the future. It assumes that these are circumstances which belong within the causal mechanism of a rain storm. The high humidity and the rapid shift in atmospheric pressure are signified by darkening clouds, windy conditions, and by an inexplicable sensation that comes through our skin which acts as a quasi-barometer.

It is important that these circumstances are observed as preceding the effect, and that they are part of an overall structure which would scientifically sanction such causal links. If such a structure is not there then either: (a) the effect was not *caused* by the preceding conditions, but merely illustrates an accident or coincidence; or (b) there is an underlying causal mechanism that science has not observed.

Conviction in possibility (b) has led to many discoveries in the history of science. Scientists have vowed to search for and explain new networks of relations which would justify tagging their observed regularity as causal. Until this is provided, however, such ascriptions are merely unproven hypotheses.

The same holds true when you move from effect to cause. These are really just two ways of looking at the same process. This process defines a close relationship between premises and conclusion (cause and effect). The nature of this connection is sometimes as a *necessary condition*. For example, oxygen is a necessary ingredient to fire. It is impossible to have a fire without it. In one sense, oxygen can be thought of as a cause of the fire.

There is another sense of cause as a *sufficient condition*. One may have oxygen and still not have a fire. Other conditions are also necessary—such as fuel and a threshold temperature. Together, these are both necessary and sufficient.

> Necessary Condition: Without the presence of some condition some specified effect will not occur.
>
> Sufficient Condition: With the addition of some condition some specified effect will occur.

Sometimes there are conditions which are sufficient and not necessary. It is sufficient to start a fire to have a book of matches and a dry newspaper. But these are not necessary for fire, because it is possible to create a fire via other means.

Try making a list of examples which present cases of: (a) a necessary condition; (b) a sufficient condition; and (c) joint necessary and sufficient conditions. These important concepts require a little work so that you may become more familiar with them.

Another aspect of cause concerns the proximity of cause to effect. In a chain of events, something far removed is less likely to be fully responsible than something closer. (A close relation will be called a "proximate cause" and a distant relation will be called a "remote cause.")

This is because in the case of a remote cause there are more intervening factors that, themselves, bear responsibility for what happens.

EXAMPLE FIVE

A. John thoughtlessly throws a cigarette butt on the dry leaves as he hikes on the trail. It catches fire and the forest burns down.

B. John thoughtlessly throws a cigarette butt on the dry leaves as he hikes on the trail. The ash is about to die out when it is fanned by Mary who keeps it alive and pours gasoline around the surrounding area. The fire grows and the forest burns down.*

In example A John is the cause of the fire because he is the proximate cause. His action directly brings about the forest fire. He is responsible and is, therefore, the cause. When we focus on who is to blame, we look to John.

In example B it is Mary who replaces John as the proximate cause. John's actions are still wrong. He is still part of the causal chain which

---

* These examples are adapted from those given by Hart and Honoré, *Causation in the Law* (Oxford: Clarendon Press, 1959), pp. 292–96, 358–61.

causes the fire. But now John shifts from being the proximate cause to being the remote cause, for if Mary had not been there (in example B), no fire would have happened. It is Mary's action which directly brings about the forest fire. She is responsible as the primary cause. When we focus on who is to blame, we look primarily to Mary. (John is still somewhat responsible as a remote cause.)

Proximate causes may be the most helpful part of the scheme for understanding *why* something happened. But remote causes are also useful. They contribute to our understanding of the larger context of *how* some effect came about.

Obviously, causal relations are a very important part of induction. Improper application of this form of induction can result in the fallacy of false cause (see Chapter Nine).

Thus, there is a need for a method to aid the practitioner in establishing general causal relations. One such group of rules was set out by the English philosopher John Stuart Mill. Mill offered five methods. We will examine four of these.

The first is called the *method of agreement*. By this method you look for examples of the given effect on a wide variety of incidents. Then you try to find the element common to each incident.

When an unusual pneumonia-like disease killed a number of American Legionnaires in Philadelphia several years ago, physicians were at a loss to discover the source of the germs and the vehicle of their distribution.

Through careful use of the method of agreement in disparate cases around the world British doctors discovered that old air-conditioning systems were a common element. From there it was discovered that excess water from the air-conditioning units had stagnated and created a perfect environment for these deadly microbes.

By examining what was common to all the cases, the mystery was solved.

Of course, this method can be abused, as in the following:

BARTENDER: Hey Joe, you're drinking quite a bit tonight.
JOE: I'm doing an experiment.
BARTENDER: Oh yeah, how's that?
JOE: I'm always getting drunk, so I'm trying to find out why.
BARTENDER: What are your results?
JOE: Well, I've had bourbon and soda, rye and soda, and scotch and soda. Now I'm drunk. The only common element among the group is the soda. Next time, I'll cut out the soda!*

In order to work correctly one must make some preliminary assumptions about the agents involved. In this case a description of what might count as a relevant similarity or difference is in order. With these cautions in mind,

* Adapted from an example given by Wesley Salmon, *Logic* (Englewood Cliffs, N.J.: Prentice-Hall, 1963), p. 112.

the method of agreement can be a powerful tool in discussing causal connections.

The second example is the *method of difference*. In this case one item is eliminated from the environment, and it is then determined whether the effect is still manifested.

This technique is often used in treating asthmatics. Asthma is a breathing disorder often triggered by allergens (particles which create an allergic reaction). The traditional method is to eliminate elements from the patient's life one by one. Each week some item is taken away such as chocolate, peaches, or feather pillows. After the item has been removed, the patient's condition is carefully monitored. If symptoms subside, then there is a good chance that the eliminated item is an offending allergen.

Again, care must be taken that when one removes an item, it is really a single unit. Otherwise we might mistake the real causal factor. For example, one asthmatic might have her mattress removed and, as a result, improve. This does not necessarily mean that the patient is allergic to the mattress itself. It is quite possible that microscopic mites which live atop all mattresses might be the offenders. If this were true, one would not have to eliminate the mattress, but merely shield the patient with a plastic mattress cover to eliminate the allergen.

Since our world is filled with interdependent collections of organisms, it is often difficult to be sure one is able to correctly follow the method of difference. This is because of the difficulty of removing one and only one variable (and keeping all external factors constant). But with careful attention to these possibilities some errors may be avoided.

The third method is called the *joint method of agreement and difference*. This is, just as the title suggests, a combination of the preceding two. By this procedure a much more sophisticated method is created that comes closer to the way we actually solve problems.

Using our example of the asthmatic again, we can illustrate the joint method as follows:

EXAMPLE SIX
JOINT METHOD

AGREEMENT		DIFFERENCE	
CONDITION	REACTION	CONDITION	REACTION
Regular foods, stuffed animals, uncovered mattress	Asthma	Covered mattress, regular foods, stuffed animals	No asthma
Special diet, stuffed animals, uncovered mattress	Asthma	No regular foods, stuffed animals, uncovered mattress	Asthma
Regular foods, no stuffed animals, uncovered mattress	Asthma	No stuffed animals, regular foods, uncovered mattress	Asthma

Comment: The joint method seeks to bring forth the necessary and sufficient conditions which are the result of employing each separate procedure. Together, they would provide a much richer sense of cause.

The joint method eliminates those sufficient conditions which are not also necessary. Obviously, the problems outlined in the practice of each method are also to be repeated here. Further, it should be stated that though the ideal is to provide necessary and sufficient conditions, these cannot be guaranteed. As in any inductive argument, the conclusions are only contingent—not only in their inherent logical status, but also because they are relative to the thoroughness of the practitioner. This last point is of no small importance. Much of the recent controversy in cancer and AIDS research has hinged upon the propriety and utility of various research strategies about which there is much disagreement.

The last method to be mentioned is that of *concomitant variation*. This method differs from the joint method, which rests upon the notion that we can totally eliminate various elements from our experimental model. However, this is not always possible. For example, if we wanted to study the causal relationship between sunspots and the concentrations of certain types of radiation in the world, then clearly the joint method would be inapplicable. We cannot eliminate sunspots. What we can do is measure the variation of radiation levels whenever sunspot activity increases or decreases. Concomitant variation seeks to show that two conditions are causally related since the variation of one leads to the variation of the other.

This method has been a powerful tool in science. Though it cannot provide necessary or sufficient conditions, it *has* been useful in discovering important causal connections between smoking and cancer; asbestos and asbestosis; sodium levels and arteriosclerosis, and so on.

Of course there is a danger that one might observe accidental correlations and from these incorrectly project a causal relationship where none exists. An example might be the asserted connection between drug addicts, homosexuals, and carriers of AIDS. Though drug addicts and homosexuals statistically have a much higher incidence of being infected than the general population, there is no essential connection between being a drug addict, a homosexual, and an AIDS victim. One becomes infected with the AIDS virus via the transfer of body fluids. This is the mode of transmission, *not* membership in some particular group. Thus, a celibate homosexual or a drug addict who always used a clean needle would be at no risk of being infected. One must not mistake the *proximate* cause with a *remote* cause even if statistics seem to correlate equally with both groups.

Since necessary and sufficient conditions are not demonstrated, there is much room for dispute about how these correlations are to be analyzed and interpreted. There is always the risk of asserting the existence of a cause where none exists.

Special Hints for Outlining Inductive Arguments

Inductive arguments can be outlined according to the general suggestions for outlining deductive arguments described in Chapter Two. The major difference between inductive and deductive arguments is that the conclusion of the latter is necessary and of the former contingent. This is also reflected in the way we check an inductive argument to determine whether it is a good one.

In the last chapter the criteria for a good deductive argument were presented: A deductive argument is good when it is *sound*. Soundness was defined as a valid argument whose premises are true. An inductive argument is good when it is *cogent*. Cogency is defined as: All inferences are highly probable (strong), and all the premises are true.

CRITERIA FOR GOOD ARGUMENTS

Sound Deductive Arguments
1. Valid inferences
2. All premises are true

Cogent Inductive Arguments
1. Strong inferences
2. All premises are true

Amendments to the Order of Logical Presentation (set out in Chapter Two)

I. Find and outline the argument (as stated in Chapter Two).
II. Test for cogency (in the case of inductive arguments).
   1. Strong inferences. Do all inductive inferences seem highly probable? Go over the fallacies for induction presented in Chapter Nine. Are the fallacies of hasty generalization, improper analogy, incomplete evidence, or false cause present? Is there anything else about the inductive inference which would cause you to doubt that it is usually true? If doubts are found, then you may use these as a basis for writing your evaluation.
   2. Are all the premises true? Go over the premises justified as 'fact' or 'assertion.' If questions about the truth of these can be raised, and the premise cannot be restated to make it true (according to the principle of fairness), then these questions should be addressed to the argument evaluation.
III. *Judgment of cogency.* If, after completing the test for cogency, one can conclude that the inferences are strong and the premises are true, then the inductive argument is cogent and its conclusions should be generally accepted.

For the rest of the process of outlining, continue according to the instructions described in Chapter Two.

EXERCISES

Directions: Identify the arguments which are inductive and those which are deductive.

GROUP A

1. Sluggo, Rocky, and Bruiser are all successful boxers. They can take a punch—and still continue fighting. Therefore, successful boxers have to be able to take a punch.

2. All viruses are distinguished by being a single strand of RNA covered with a protein coat. This unknown organism before us is simply a single strand of RNA covered by a protein coat. This unknown organism is a virus.

3. Most societies have sanctions against murder. The Hopi constitute a small society. The Hopi have a sanction against murder.

4. The gears on my automobile do not disengage easily. There is a popping noise occasionally when I depress the clutch. Pretty soon my clutch cable is going to break.

5. Whenever it rains all hydrophobic organisms stay under cover. Right now it's raining. Let's go out and enjoy ourselves. There's no chance of getting rabies today.

GROUP B

1. Edward Jenner noted that Sarah Portlock, Mary Barge, Elizabeth Wynne, Simon Nichols, Joseph Merret, and William Rodway had all suffered cowpox, and they seemed not to be infected by smallpox in cases he might have expected. To be sure, he inoculated them with smallpox directly. Nothing happened. Years passed and he repeated his observation. These people were immune. Jenner concluded that it was the cowpox which made them immune.

2. Yellow Fever is an acute infection that creates a deep jaundiced condition. Other symptoms include dizziness, rapid onset of fever, headache, nausea, and vomiting. Death may occur on the sixth or seventh day of illness and has been known to occur in as many as 50 percent of those infected. During the Spanish-American War, Walter Reed was sent to Cuba to solve the problem. Reed narrowed the correlative antecedents from a large to a small list.

     The possible candidates for the cause of Yellow Fever were: (a) mosquitoes who had fed on infected victims; (b) excreta of Yellow Fever patients; (c) dishes and silver of patients; and (d) clothing of patients. Reed built a mosquito-proof building and divided the interior space in two. One space contained mosquitoes who had fed on Yellow Fever victims. The other space was left alone. Nonimmune volunteers were put in each half of the building. Volunteers in the mosquito side contracted the disease.

     Next, the other items on the list were given to volunteers in a similarly constructed setting. One by one, and then in concert, these other factors failed to bring on the illness. Thus, by breaking up the list and eliminating each factor one by one, it was determined that mosquitoes alone transmitted the disease.

ARGUMENTS ON COGENCY

Directions: In the following exercises decide which of these inductive arguments are cogent and why.

1. It is election night and Mrs. Johnson is ahead with 50 percent of the vote reported. Mrs. Johnson is sure to be elected.
2. My horoscope is usually right. Today it says I should be prepared to take financial risks. Therefore, I withdrew all the money from my bank account and am waiting.
3. In the months after our cat died I suddenly realized that the indoor plants—which had always been scrawny—were now blooming in health. Nothing else in our apartment had changed. I'll bet our cat bothered them by eating leaves and scratching the stems.
4. The army trains its soldiers well in boot camp. Thus, these soldiers are ready for everything real war has to dish out.
5. "The only one who could have committed the murder is the person who had access to the murder weapon, had a motive, and was near the room where the crime was committed. You did it, Professor Plum! You killed Colonel Mustard with a lead pipe in the study."
   —imaginary detective solving his case

READING QUESTIONS

1. What is enumerative induction?
2. What is induction by analogy?
3. What is the difference between necessary and sufficient conditions?
4. State four of Mill's methods.
5. What are the criteria for good deductive and inductive arguments?

CHAPTER FOUR

Pictorial argument

One of the most common forms of persuasion we are confronted with is that of advertising. In today's society advertising plays an increasingly larger role in our lives. The purpose of advertising is to persuade a segment of people about an idea, product, or service. Many people make a number of very important decisions based upon these advertisements. Therefore, it seems appropriate to present an application of persuasion and argument in one of its forms: advertising—especially through visual ads which I will call *pictorial argument*.

ADVERTISER AND PRODUCT IMAGES

Like all other instantiations of argument, pictorial argument employs the *elements within the context of argument* (see Introduction).

These work together to create a communications flow, as illustrated in Table Five. As in all other arguments, the advertisement seeks to promote some intended purpose. This can represent a product or the advertiser itself. The difference between these is readily apparent.

Advertiser image. The company or political candidate wishes to promote itself. This can include enhancing the firm's image or reputation. The logical principle behind this is similar to the inductive principle known as Mill's principle of agreement (described in the last chapter). If we say that customer satisfaction among all car models is highest with Ford, then we are declaring that the Ford Automobile Company is the common causal

TABLE FIVE: Elements of a Pictorial Argument Context

ADVERTISER (SPEAKER)	PURPOSE (POINT OF CONTENTION)	ADVERTISEMENT (ARGUMENT)	MESSAGE RECEPTION (COMMON BODY OF KNOWLEDGE)	SEGMENT OF PUBLIC (AUDIENCE)
Company, political candidate, and so on	$\left\{\begin{array}{l}\text{Corporate Image}\\\text{Product Image}\end{array}\right.$ $\downarrow$ Positive Image	Message placed in magazine, newspaper, radio, TV, and so on	Assumed knowledge, attitudes, and so forth needed to receive intended message	Specific market for whom ad is intended
		$\longrightarrow$		
		Communications Flow		

feature and thus *all* its products have a high probability of producing satisfaction.

PRODUCT	REACTION
Ford Mustang	High Satisfaction
Ford Taurus	High Satisfaction
Ford Fiesta	High Satisfaction

Common Factor = Ford

∴ Ford cars tend to produce customer satisfaction.

Of course there is no *certainty* that just because overall satisfaction is high that it is therefore high on each and every model. The point of promoting the advertiser's image is precisely to build public confidence in the producer, in general, and by extension in its products. Such confidence is important. A competent company is an important ingredient, though not a necessary or a sufficient condition for producing good products.

Product image.   Unless we are thinking of acquiring or buying stock in a company, most of us are more interested in the product itself. Why should we buy this type of product at all? Why should we buy the product from Acme Corporation? There are two important purposes of product promotion. If the product to be sold is a car telephone, then the first task may be to convince people they need car telephones, and then, secondly, that the company's product does a better job meeting that need than any other.

The advertisement itself seeks to fulfill this purpose. It creates a logical argument or logical fallacy to fulfill this goal. This is accomplished by making certain assumptions about the segment of the public to which the ad is directed. These assumptions might include the interests and educational level of the intended market.

Fig. 4–1

Advertisement used by permission, courtesy of Rosenthal, Greene and Campbell

Together, these elements create a successful ad which persuades. Let us see how this works in the example shown in Figure 4-1.

OUTLINING THE ARGUMENT

Comment: In this ad the advertiser is Presidential Airlines. The *purpose* is to get people to fly this airline to selected cities (product image).

The argument runs something like this:

1. We all have a limited amount of money to spend on a vacation. (*assertion*)
2. Getting to our destination is not a focus of the vacation. (*assertion*)
3. Enjoying events at our destination is what we most desire. (*assertion*)
4. Spending less on transport frees more money to spend on other aspects of our vacation. (*corollary from 1*)
5. Most of us would rather spend money on other aspects of our vacation than on transport. (*1–4*)
6. Presidential's fares are low. (*fact*)
7. Flying Presidential allows us to spend more on our vacation. (*4, 6*)
8. When one vacation budget category is lowered, most people will take this windfall of money and spend it on luxuries that are desired but not essential. (*assertion*)
9. Being able to purchase luxuries is a desirable part of a vacation. (*assertion*)
10. Flying Presidential allows one to purchase desirable vacation luxuries. (*7–9*)
11. Flying Presidential allows one to better enjoy a vacation by enabling one to spend more on nontransport costs including desirable luxuries. (*5, 10*)

The Presidential Airlines advertisement creates this argument using three devices: (a) an assertion about allocating money for vacations; (b) factual information about Presidential's fares; and (c) a pictorial representation of various luxuries that one might desire to purchase—but couldn't unless he were shown a way to come into a windfall. The "windfall" is the money you save by flying Presidential. This extra money can be used for high-class recreation such as golf, fine dining, the theatre, shopping, or in any other manner.

This ad only appeals to a certain market segment: those people who take vacations to cities distant enough to require air transportation and who enjoy upgrade luxuries even though they are constrained by a budget. This market is described in (a) above. The assumed circumstances of this market segment constitute the common body of knowledge necessary for the reception of the message. This assumed body of knowledge defines the market and makes possible the intended message to the consumer.

In this way we can fill in the classification from Table Five, as shown in Table Six.

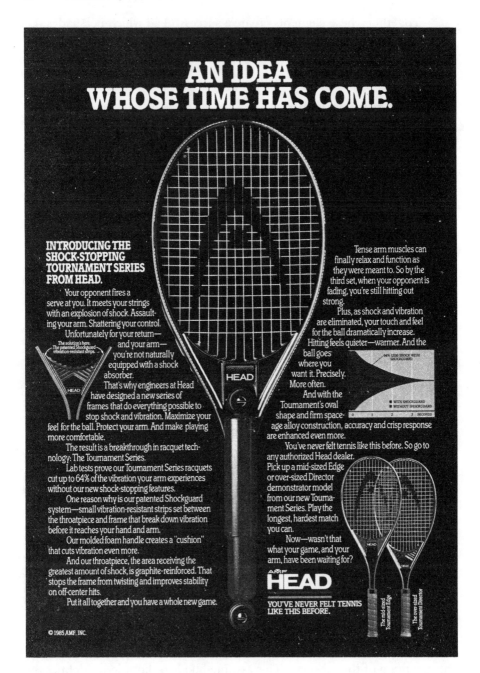

Fig. 4–2

Advertisement used by permission, courtesy of Earle Palmer Brown Companies

TABLE SIX: Example of a Pictorial Argument Context

ADVERTISER (SPEAKER)	PURPOSE (POINT OF CONTENTION)	ADVERTISEMENT (ARGUMENT)	MESSAGE RECEPTION (COMMON BODY OF KNOWLEDGE)	SEGMENT OF PUBLIC (AUDIENCE)
Presidential Airways	Fly Presidential for your summer vacation	Eleven-step argument can be outlined from pictorial argument	Defined in steps 1 through 5 and 8 through 9 of the logical outline	−Those people requiring air transport for vacation −Who enjoy upgrade luxuries −Who are on a budget

Communications Flow

Thus pictorial argument can be a legitimate form of persuasion that operates on the same principles as other forms of logical argument. It can be outlined and evaluated according to the same rules presented in this volume.

At the same time, pictorial argument is also subject to logical fallacy. Some advertisements may engage in false or misleading statements as a ploy to gain business. This necessitates a wary and careful consumer approach. Since all of us at one time or another will be among those in a market to whom an advertisement is directed, it is important to hone our skills of logical analysis so that we might be able to use advertisements as helpful purveyors of information. By understanding the logical content of the ad we can evaluate its merits and demerits within a framework that permits us to retain our autonomy.

READING QUESTIONS

1. Find a pictorial ad and outline the argument.
2. Put your ad into a larger context as in Tables Five and Six.
3. Can you name some other ordinary examples of argument we confront daily? How can outlining help us?
4. Analyze the following ad according to form presented in this chapter (see Figure 4-2).

CHAPTER FIVE

First steps

Now we are ready to begin actual outlines. This short chapter has two sets of practical exercises designed to help you write successful logical outlines. These two skill areas are often identified as stumbling blocks by those beginning the process of reconstructing arguments in outline form. They are: (a) identifying the conclusions and the premises, and (b) using suppressed premises. Skill in these two areas will be of great use in setting out your first outlines (Chapter Six).

IDENTIFYING CONCLUSIONS AND PREMISES

The most common problem in reconstructing arguments in the form of a logical outline is determining just what is a premise and what is a conclusion. Often the text appears opaque and one struggles to find its structure. As mentioned earlier, one must first discover the conclusion. The best way to do this is by becoming sensitive to the thematic context. Ask yourself key questions after reading a passage, such as, "Why did the author write this?", "What was the author's intention?", and "What was the author trying to prove?"

If these questions do not point you to something immediately, then try two other tricks: (a) Pretend you are a reporter writing a story on the author's ideas. What would make a good headline for your feature? (b) Pretend you are an attorney in a trial. The author is the opposing attorney and is making a case before the jury. You must discover the main point of the opposing argument so you can respond.

These questions and imaginary situations are merely devices to help one become sensitive to the thematic context. This context, including what comes before and after, can place one in the proper interpretative position to ascertain with confidence the point of contention.

From the thematic context the conclusion should readily become clear. It is the *point of the passage*. Once this has been determined one can ask, "How is this point being supported?", "What is the proof?", and other such questions. The answers to these questions should supply the premises of the argument, providing the reasons for accepting the point of the passage.

If these questions do not work, try imagining the following situations: (a) You are a reporter and you must set down *why* the author felt the way he or she did and *how* he or she intended to make others believe the point of contention. (b) You are a lawyer and before you can set out your case, you have to know the basis of your opponent's case.

All of the above suggestions merely represent ways to get at the main point of an argument and its accompanying support. The reader is encouraged to think of other methods that might work. Try these in exercises which follow this section of the chapter.

In short, the preferred method is:

THEMATIC CONTEXT

a.   The point of the passage = conclusion.
b.   Reasons for accepting the point of the passage = premises.

If you are still baffled by some passage, then you may want to see if any verbal clues exist. Verbal clues are key words which often signify conclusions or premises. These words are signals that can be useful when all else fails.

For example, the following words and phrases often indicate a conclusion:

> therefore, hence, thus, consequently, so, it follows that, it must be that, we may infer that, necessarily, now we can see that, it is now evident that, shows that, indicates that, proves that, entails that, implies that, establishes that, or allows us to believe that.

What follows these words is generally a conclusion. If these words occur near the beginning or end of a paragraph, it is likely that this is the conclusion of the argument contained within the entire paragraph. (Of course, some arguments continue for several paragraphs or pages.)

The following words and phrases generally signify the presence of a premise:

> because, so, since, in order to, for the reason that, for, assuming that, is shown by, is indicated by, is proven by, is entailed by, is implied by, is established by, in that, due to the fact that, given that, may be concluded from, inasmuch as.

What follows these words is generally a premise or a group of premises.

The word 'so' can tip off either a conclusion or a premise depending on how it is used as in the following:

'So' as premise indicator: We'll buy eggs today so we don't have to go the store tomorrow, which is a holiday.

'So' as a conclusion indicator: It is raining. We hate getting wet, so let's take an umbrella.

In the sample argument in Chapter Two there is only one verbal clue: therefore. None of the premises are marked either; thus, verbal clues are not always present. They represent one final way to determine the argumentative structure when the primary method, thematic context, has failed.

If one is unsure about a difficult passage in which he has tried the thematic context method and in which there are no word clues, try substituting a word from the appropriate list where you think it might function. This requires making a guess and then inserting the word clue to confirm or disconfirm this hypothesis.

For example, consider this passage:

Maggie became skinny. She had suffered an emotional loss over the death of her father and food no longer tasted good to her.

Guess at the conclusion: Maggie became skinny.
Confirmation with word clues: 'because' after the conclusion should indicate premises.

Maggie became skinny *because* she had suffered an emotional loss over the loss of her father and food no longer tasted good.

New paragraph makes sense: therefore the hypothesis is confirmed.
Resulting outline: 1. Maggie suffered an emotional loss over her father's death. (*fact*)
2. Food no longer tasted good to Maggie. (*fact*)
3. Maggie lost weight. (*1, 2*)

This last approach is called the mixed mode. It is used when one cannot fully determine premises and conclusions by the thematic context method, and there are no word clues.

A summary of these three methods follows:

Best method: thematic context. The point of the passage is the conclusion. The reasons for accepting the point of the passage are called the premises.
Alternate 1: word clues. These are various words and phrases which often signal the presence of premises and conclusions.
Alternate 2: mixed mode. In difficult passages in which the context does not help to positively identify premises and conclusions in which there are no

word clues try substituting some of the word clues into crucial sections of the text. If the sense remains the same, then the inserted words will help you identify premises and conclusions.

EXERCISES

Directions: Identify the conclusion and the premises.

GROUP A

1. China is the largest country in the world. America can use all the allies it can get. Thus, America should cultivate China's friendship and support.

2. "The road less taken" has made all the difference because I am not a man whose nature it is to follow the crowd, and the other road represents the direction that most people choose. It makes all the difference when you are true to your nature.

3. Dan Marino will be one of the top quarterbacks in NFL history, assuming that he remains as productive in the future as he has been in the past and that the quarterback rating system is a true indicator of a quarterback's relative talent. Up to now Marino is near the top of the NFL's quarterback rating system.

4. Terrorists, by definition, are murderers since they prey upon innocent civilians who are not directly involved with their dispute. People who kill innocents are murderers. Libya continues to support terrorists and those who support some group must take some responsibility for that group's actions. Consequently, Libya's leaders must share in the responsibility for terrorist incidents.

GROUP B

1. Robert Redford is a great film star. He has starred with famous talents such as Paul Newman, Barbra Streisand, Mia Farrow, and Jane Fonda. Redford's films have always made money and drawn critical acclaim. Who would deny the attraction he holds over women of all ages? These are the markings of a true star.

2. "High tech" expertise is the highest demonstration of human knowledge. Today, civilization has achieved a level of "high tech" expertise that is unmatched in history. Truly, we are the most brilliant group of humans in history.

—declaration of a former student

3. No one wants the world to end. But just as true, no one wants our country to be conquered by military force. Disarmament talks involve a difficult balancing act. The stakes are high. But something must be done to represent both poles of opinion.

4. Most of the Interstate Highway System has roadways that were designed to handle traffic going 80 MPH. We should raise the speed limits on the Interstate Highway System. What a waste to drive 55 MPH on roads designed to be navigated safely at 80 MPH! The gas savings at 55 are minimal. Besides, no one obeys this law anyway. And laws which no one obeys breed disrespect for law in general; nobody wants that.

—paraphrase of a popular argument

USING SUPPRESSED PREMISES

Suppressed premises, or enthymemes, exist because it is often cumbersome to set out each and every premise in a prose argument. Certain points that seem trivial, or are easily supplied by the mind, are generally omitted.

If, for example, a mayoral candidate said, "Experience counts; vote for John Doe," the suppressed premise would be "John Doe has experience." Without this premise the argument is invalid, but the suppressed premise is easily supplied by the mind.

However, as we will see in Chapter Nine, the possibility of logical fallacy requires an active level of vigilance. It is easy to be fooled when the stated argument becomes complicated. Thus, there is a necessity to be exact in the reconstruction of persuasive argument; including suppressed premises.

Sometimes people express anxiety over the fact that they feel they are pulling suppressed premises out of "thin air." They feel that such a procedure is too random and undermines the objective character of the argument.

To these people I reply that not *any* additional premise will be allowed, but only those that: (a) meet a formally observed inferential gap; (b) are in the spirit of the general argument; and (c) do not contradict any other avowed position of the author. By observing these three cautions one can avoid misrepresenting the author by substituting one's own argument for the author's.

In trying to meet these three requirements ask yourself, "What is necessary to complete this argument?" If you can make the substitution observing the above cautions, do so. It is only by representing complete arguments that we can accurately determine whether or not they are correct.

Note: As a matter of form, put suppressed premises into brackets so that others will understand that these are your additions.

1. Experience counts. (*assertion*)
2. John Doe has experience. (*fact*)]
3. Vote for John Doe. (*1, 2*)

EXERCISES

Directions: Supply the missing sentence whether it is a premise or conclusion. Put your missing sentence in brackets.

GROUP A

1. No enthymemes are complete, so this argument is incomplete.

2. Ezra Pound made fascist broadcasts. Therefore, after the war he was imprisoned.
3. I have two tickets for the game tonight. We like each other and we like basketball.
4. Only members may use this tennis court. You will have to go away.
5. You can't borrow my car. I only lend it to good drivers.
6. Abortion means you have killed a fetus. Abortion is impermissible.
7. Abortion means a woman has made a choice about her body. Abortion is permissible.

GROUP B

1. Lovers may never possess all of another's love, for to be a lover is fervently to desire possessing all of another's love. But the heart daily grows in its capacity to love.

   —adapted from "Lovers Infiniteness" by John Donne

2. Fred says that he believes in every word in the Bible exactly as it is written. Further, Fred claims that every Christian must serve God. One thing that is written is that Man cannot serve both God and Mammon. It follows that Fred is not a Christian.

3. Orestes: You don't see them, you don't—but I see them: they are hunting me down . . . hence the soul cannot be possessed of the divine union, until it is divested itself of the love of created beings.

   —from "Sweeney Agonistes" by T. S. Eliot

   (Hint: Orestes' soul is not divested of the love of created beings.)

CHAPTER SIX

Exercises in outlining

This chapter presents small sections of text and pictorial argument—all of which contain arguments. These arguments are drawn from contemporary life and the history of ideas. In each case a section of text is presented. The section should be read and outlined according to the rules set out in the preceding chapters. In some cases there may be more than one argument. These may be combined into a single argument, set out as a chain, or put down as separate arguments. At the end of the book the conclusions for the major arguments are given to aid those readers who may be having trouble mastering an argument.

In lieu of working the examples in this chapter, your teacher may direct you to practice on the normal readings for the class. This option allows the rules of outlining to be applied to practical tasks and enhances the mastery of the term's readings.

One final note: Save your completed outlines as these same sections will serve as material for the exercises in evaluation.

CONTEMPORARY LIFE

1. From: A. J. Bayer, President, A.B.C. Trash, Inc.
   To: B. O. Doyle, Vice-president of Marketing and Sales
   Re: Slump in sales for A.B.C.'s "Mighty Trash Bag"

   In the past twelve months our market share of plastic trash bags has dropped from 18 percent to 14 percent. As you know, during this period there has been a large influx of cheap, generic quality trash bags that sell for twenty-five to fifty cents less per ten-bag gross. This trend has got to change.

We need a campaign to spur sales. We are the highest-priced trash bag, but we are also the best. Doesn't anybody care what they put their trash out in? Don't they care if the bag breaks on the way to the can, or if it's so thin that everyone in the neighborhood can see their garbage? These are powerful points in our favor. Try to sell them to the public or I'll be writing memos to someone else.

2. See Figure 6-1.

3. In recent days . . . men of note have been confronted, separately, with choices between speaking out in public or ducking. . . . Mr. [Drew] Lewis, who is now chairman of Union Pacific Railroad Co., was at his alma mater, Haverford College, to receive an honorary degree. In what has become a familiar ritual at such events, some faculty members and students took exception to the decision that had somehow been reached to honor him. Their reason was his role in breaking the air traffic controllers' strike in the early part of the first Reagan term. On Friday before the Sunday commencement, the faculty members sent a letter of protest to the college's acting president. On Sunday some students passed out leaflets containing the faculty statement, and some wore white armbands as a sign of their dissent.

As such things go, it was a decorous expression. It nonetheless wounded Mr. Lewis—who responded by shrugging out of his ceremonial hood and handing back his degree. Haverford has Quaker roots. The Quaker tradition leans in its gentle but insistent way toward composing differences rather than displaying them, and Mr. Lewis invoked this in his remarks. "I believe in consensus," he is reported to have said. "There is no consensus on this degree when one-third of your faculty objects. With great respect for the college, I return the degree."

He received a standing ovation. The school is now embarrassed, and rightly so. Too often over the years, it has been the other way around. Colleges neither are nor should be orderly places. They are diverse and highly imaginative communities. But at some point a community must stand for something—and its disappointed members acquiesce in the result—or it stands for nothing. Decide; then honor your decision. That seemed to be part of what Mr. Lewis stood up to say, and not just for himself. Not a bad rule.

—copyright © *Washington Post,* May 21, 1986

4. See Figure 6-2.

5. Representative Neil Abercrombie took the oath of office last month in the waning days of the 99th Congress and is probably its only member to suffer a pang of despair over his election. Abercrombie lost the 20 September Democratic primary in Hawaii's 1st District. But he was awakened the next day with the news that he had won a special election held the same day to serve out the House term of former Democratic Representative Cecil Heftel, who resigned to run for governor.

The news of victory brought "a little bit of despair, a kind of sinking feeling," says Abercrombie, a Democrat who was sworn in on 23 September 1986 for a term that will end 3 January 1987. "Perhaps more than any other person here, I had to think very hard on what Thomas Jefferson said about political honor: that it is a splendid torment," Abercrombie said in an interview last week in his bare-walled office in the Longworth House Office Building.

A hand-painted sign bearing the new congressman's name is posted outside his office, but Abercrombie said he hopes the House printers will make up an official sign before Congress adjourns for the year—probably

Fig. 6-1

Advertisement used by permission, courtesy of Earle Palmer Brown Companies

50

Fig. 6–2

Advertisement used by permission, courtesy of Earle Palmer Brown Companies

"I've never seen a better arrangement of space."
— Copernicus, famous scientist

It's hard to beat 33,655 square feet of flexible meeting space. All so expertly arranged that we have two ballrooms situated adjacent to each other.

At the Crystal Gateway Marriott, we can arrange meetings for up to 2,000 people. And with the new Arlington Tower opening in 1987, we'll also be able to offer 700 luxurious guest rooms — making our hotel the newest addition to the Marriott Convention Network.

So call (703) 920-3230 and book your next meeting with us. Ask about the free welcoming reception, too. But hurry — because space is going quickly.

CRYSTAL GATEWAY Marriott.
1700 Jefferson Davis Hwy,
Arlington, VA 22202

BETTMANN ARCHIVE

Fig. 6–3

Advertisement used by permission, courtesy of Rosenthal, Greene and Campbell this week. Receptionist Marilyn Bruce, one of several former Heftel aides staying on for the rest of the term, says she still has trouble announcing the new congressman's name when she picks up the phone. . . .

Abercrombie said, "I came up here with all of the responsibility and presumably all the authority of a member of Congress but with a tenure so brief that I will have to take the consequences of my votes without being able to participate to any great degree other than by the vote itself."

—from "Hawaii Congressman to Serve Three-Month Term," by James Rowley. Copyright © Associated Press.

6. See Figure 6-3.

HISTORY OF IDEAS

1. Tragedy has all the elements of epic poetry. It can use dactylic hexameter, and has no small amount of music and visual concreteness through which its inherent pleasure is made most vivid. Tragedy has vividness both when it is read as well as when it is acted.

Further, tragedy accomplishes its end with greater economy of length. What is more compact is more pleasant than that which is long, drawn out. Suppose, for example, that Sophocles' *Oedipus Tyrannus* should be as long as the *Iliad!*

Again, an epic imitation is less of a unity than a tragedy. This is shown through the fact that one epic provides material for several tragedies. Moreover, if epic poets ever do use a single plot, the resulting poem seems truncated if they treat it briefly, or if they treat it with epic fullness, it seems thin. . . . If, then, tragedy is superior to epic in all these respects and also in accomplishing its artistic purpose . . . it is evidently superior to epic poetry since it achieves its purpose better.

—Aristotle, *Poetics* 1462^a–1462^b

2. Liberty? The true liberty of a man, you would say, consisted in his finding out, or being forced to find out the right path, and to walk thereon. To learn, or to be taught, what work he actually was able for; and then by permission, persuasion, and even compulsion, to set about doing of the same! That is his true blessedness, honour, 'liberty,' and maximum of wellbeing: if liberty be not that, I for one have small care about liberty. You do not allow a palpable madman to leap over precipices; you violate his liberty, you that are wise; and keep him, were it in strait-waistcoats, away from the precipices! Every stupid, every cowardly and foolish man is but a less palpable madman: His true liberty were that a wiser man, that any and every wiser man, could by brass collars, or in whatever milder or sharper way, lay hold of him when he was going wrong, and order and compel him to go a little righter. O, if thou really art my Senior, Seigneur, my Elder, Presbyter, or Priest—if thou art in very deed my Wiser, may a beneficent instinct lead and impel thee to 'conquer' me, to command me! If thou do

know better than I what is good and right, I conjure thee in the name of God, force me to do it; were it by never such brass collars, whips, and handcuffs, leave me not to walk over precipices! That I have been called by all the Newspapers a "free man" will avail me little, if my pilgrimage have ended in death and wreck. O that the Newspapers had called me slave, coward, fool, or what it pleased their sweet voices to name me, and I had attained not death, but life—Liberty requires new definitions.

—Thomas Carlyle, *Past and Present*

3. It is foolish and inconsistent to say, "I would prefer not to be rather than be unhappy." The man who says, "I prefer this to that," chooses *something;* but "not to be" is not *something,* but *nothing.* Therefore, one cannot rightly choose when he opts for something that does not exist. One should say that he wished to exist although he was unhappy. But someone might declare that this is not his wish. Rather, he wishes not to exist. You answer, but if you ought to have willed not to exist, then "not to exist" is better. However, what does not exist cannot be better; therefore, you should not have willed this. The feeling through which you do not will not to exist is more authentic than the opinion by which you think that you ought to will not to exist.

Furthermore, a man necessarily becomes better when he fulfills a proper choice. He who does not exist, however, cannot be better. No one, therefore, can rightly choose not to exist.

—Saint Augustine, *On the Free Choice of the Will,* Book Three, Chapter 8, 76–78

4. I have just persuaded myself that nothing at all exists in the world: no sky, no earth, no minds, and no bodies. Have I thus convinced myself that I also did not exist? Not at all. Clearly, I existed if I was persuaded of something or even if I thought anything at all. For though there may be a deceiver of some sort, quite powerful and crafty, who is intent on keeping me perpetually deceived, there can be no slightest doubt that I exist, since he deceives *me.* Let him deceive me as much as he wants, he can never make me be nothing as long as I think that I am something. Thus, after my careful, considered judgment on the subject, I must finally conclude this proposition: *I am, I exist,* is necessarily true every time that I pronounce it or conceive it in my mind.

—Rene Descartes, *Meditations on First Philosophy,* Meditation 2

5. But the communication of pleasure may be the immediate object of a work not metrically composed; and that object may have been in a high degree attained, as in novels and romances. Would then the mere superaddition of metre, with or without rhyme, entitle *these* to the name of poems? The answer is that nothing can permanently please, which does not contain in itself the reason why it is so, and not otherwise. If metre be superadded, all other parts must be made consonant with it. They must be such as to

justify the perpetual and distinct attention to each part, which an exact correspondent recurrence of accent and sound are calculated to excite. The final definition then, so deduced, may be thus worded. A poem is that species of composition which is opposed to works of science by proposing for its *immediate* object pleasure, not truth; and from all other species (having *this* object in common with it) it is discriminated by proposing to itself such delight from the *whole,* as is compatible with a distinct gratification from each component *part.*

—Samuel Taylor Coleridge, *Biographia Literaria,* Ch. 14

6. An example of an indirect argument.

S: Tell me, then, what kind of action is pious and what kind is impious? . . .

E: Well, the pious is what the gods love and what isn't is impious.

S: Good, Euthyphro. This is the sort of answer I wanted. We will see whether it is true, but clearly you will see to that.

E: Certainly.

S: Well, let's examine the meaning of your definition. An action or man which the gods love is pious, but an action or man hated by the gods is impious. They are not the same, but quite opposite: the pious and the impious. True?

E: Quite.

S: I've properly stated it?

E: Yes.

S: We have already stated that sometimes the gods are in a state of disagreement. In these cases they are at odds with each other, and in these situations there is enmity between them.

E: True.

S: What are the subject areas that cause such discord with hatred and anger? Let's view it in this way. If you and I were to disagree about numbers and which is greater, would this produce such enmity and make us enemies, or would we proceed to count and soon resolve our difference about this?

E: The latter.

S: Again, if we differed about the larger and the smaller, wouldn't we resort to measurement to resolve our conflict?

E: Yes.

S: And about the heavier and the lighter, wouldn't we resort to weighing and become reconciled?

E: Naturally.

S: What subject would make us angry if we were unable to resolve it? Perhaps you aren't prepared to say just yet, but examine as I suggest whether these would be the types of topic areas: the just and unjust; the beautiful and ugly; the good and bad. Aren't these controversial subjects about which there is often no accord and as a result of which enmity and discord follow?

E: You have the distinction between the two subject areas correct, Socrates.

S: What about the gods, Euthyphro? If indeed they have differences, will they not also be about these topic areas?

E: Certainly.

S: Then according to the argument, my good Euthyphro, different gods consider different things to be just, beautiful, ugly, good, and bad, for they would not be at odds unless it were concerning these subjects.

E: Correct.

S: And they love what each of them considers beautiful, good, and just and hate the opposites?

E: Yes.

S: But you say that the same things are considered just by some gods and unjust by others and since they dispute these sorts of subjects, they are at odds and at war with each other. True?

E: Yes.

S: The same things are loved by the gods and hated by the gods and would be god-loved and god-hated.

E: It seems that way.

S: And the same things would be both pious and impious, according to this argument?

E: I guess so.

S: Then, you haven't answered my original question.

—Plato, *Euthyphro*, 7ᵃ–8ᵇ

CHAPTER SEVEN

What is an evaluation?

An evaluation is a reasoned response to a logical argument. This reasoned response takes a point of view that can be seen as supporting the argument or not. The former response will be called a "pro" evaluation and the latter a "con" evaluation. Chapter Eight will concentrate on the mechanics of how to construct each. This chapter will give an overview of some of the elements which make up this form of argumentation.

The first thing an evaluation needs is structure. Without structure, by which its remarks may be guided, an evaluation becomes meaningless. As was said earlier about movies (see Introduction), general statements which do not make their measurement scale explicit yield no useful information. Sometimes they are worse than nothing because they *can* make things more unclear.

An evaluation must: (a) make clear the assessed character of that which is being evaluated (an argument, book, opera, movie, and so on); (b) analyze that character into its components; (c) direct attention to particular important components; (d) put forth a point of view directed through those components; (e) generate a reasoned argument for that point of view; and (f) show how one's view of the whole is affected by the positions taken on those components.

This is a tall order. Let us examine in a little more detail some of these points. The first two have been covered in Chapter Two under *The Order of Logical Presentation*. They dictate, in the case of an argumentative text, that a logical outline be formed.

DECIDING WHICH PREMISES TO FOCUS UPON

Once there is an outline, one must examine the various premises beginning with those justified by "assertion." Assertion is the weakest form of justification; therefore, one is most likely to find the particular, important component toward which the reader wishes to direct attention.

What is especially important at this point is to view such premises in a *pluralistic context*. This is a context in which many viewpoints regarding that single element might be brought forth. It is very important that one not allow a strong personal feeling to mask all the possible reasons one might be inclined to accept or reject this particular premise. The reason for this pluralism is that it allows a more comprehensive vision of the assertion.

You cannot know why you are for or against a single tenet until you understand fully all the various reasons others give for their assent or dissent. Thus, this pluralistic appraisal of the premise is extremely important in developing an informed view on its truth or falsity.

Obviously, such a process is time consuming. One must limit the number of premises under consideration. The two guides that should rule such a choice are: (a) the crucial nature of the premise, and (b) the controversial nature of the premise. These guides act serially; in other words, we apply (a) before (b). One needs first to examine that premise(s) that is crucial to the argument. Is it correct or not? If the reviewer is in any doubt, he should apply the pluralism principle in order to help him decide.

Among several *crucial* premises that may be isolated, the *controversial* nature of a premise should narrow one's choice. This is because one will need to more fully develop a position on such a premise since it is the one to which most reviewers will naturally gravitate.

An example of this can be seen in the following argument:

1. Children develop best when they spend large quantities (fourteen or more hours daily) of well-used time with their parents. (*assertion*)
2. Parents have an obligation to provide their children with the best possibilities for development. (*assertion*)
3. Parents have an obligation to spend large quantities of well-used time with their children. (*1, 2*)
4. No one can maintain a full-time outside career while spending fourteen or more hours a day on child care. (*fact*)
5. Parents have an obligation to provide at least minimum clothing, shelter, and food to their children. (*assertion*)
6. Children need a minimum of clothing, shelter, and food before they need anything else. (*assertion*)
7. When one parent cannot provide minimum clothing, shelter, and food, both parents must work. (*5, 6*)
8. Beyond the minimum amount of material goods, parental nurturing is more important than greater amounts of material goods. (*assertion*)

9. When one parent can provide at least the minimum clothing, shelter, and food, the other parent should stay home to rear the child. (*3, 4, 8*)

10. The number of parents who work outside the home should depend solely upon whether that family needs a second income to provide the minimum necessities of life. (*7, 9*)

In this argument there are several assertions.

1. Children develop best when they spend large quantities of well-used time with their parents.
2. Parents have an obligation to provide their children with the best possibilities for development.
5. Parents have an obligation to provide at least minimum clothing, shelter, and food to their children.
6. Children need a minimum of clothing, shelter, and food before they need anything else.
8. Beyond the minimum of material goods, nurturing by a parent is more important than greater amounts of material goods.

According to the two criteria above we must first examine the crucial premises and then the controversial ones. In this argument premises 1 and 2, 5 and 6, and 8 stand out as groups on the same topic.

Crucial Premises

Crucial premises **are those which are the most fundamental. One sentence is more fundamental than another when it is logically prior.**

Between premises 1 and 2, the most crucial is the first. This is because premise 1 establishes a particular need. Throughout the argument it is assumed that parents should fulfill the legitimate needs of their children. Therefore, it is crucial to establish these needs. The needs are logically prior to their satisfaction. The legitimate need establishes a cause. The parents' reaction is the effect. Cause is prior to effect. If one can show a legitimate need, then one has shown that it should be satisfied. The question is: What is a legitimate need? Premise 1 purports to show just such a need.

By the same reasoning, premise 6 is more essential than premise 5 since premise 6 also establishes a need. Thus, we have shown that premises 1, 6, and 8 are the most crucial by means of examining logical priority and cause and effect.

Other methods available for accomplishing this function include an examination of the argument's inferential structure. By paying careful attention to the interlocking structure and the vehicle of each individual inference, some of the priority relations may become clear.

TABLE SEVEN: The Controversial Premise

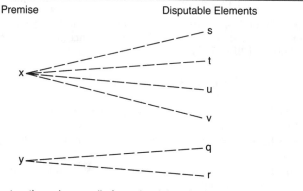

Premise	Disputable Elements

(If elements s through r are all of equal weight, x is more controversial than y.)

Controversial Premises

After examining the crucial nature of the premises, one must decide which are the most controversial. The candidates for this choice come from our exercise on crucial premises.

1. Children develop best when they spend large quantities of well-used time with their parents.
6. Children need a minimum of clothing, shelter, and food before they need anything else.
8. Beyond the minimum of material goods, parental nurturing is more important than greater amounts of material goods.

Which of these is controversial? Clearly, few would disagree with the truth of premise 6: If we were not provided with the bare necessities of life, we would die. Thus, this assertion seems well supported by scientific fact.

The remaining choices are premises 1 and 8. Before any decision can be made, more amplification of "controversial" is needed. The primary meaning, of course, refers to a point of dispute. But the etymology suggests a metaphorical connotation of various aspects of a premise turning against the premise itself. Thus, a more controversial premise is the one that has more parts that could potentially be turned against it. In Table Seven, x is more controversial than y because x has four elements which could be turned against it, as opposed to two for y. Obviously, this rule is meant to be a general guide rather than an exact quantitative measurement. The analysis into elements is only approximate at best. But the principle allows one some guidance in making a selection between several candidates.

Still, there may be times when y is chosen over x. This might be the

TABLE EIGHT: Judging the Controversial Premise of the Sample

PREMISE   ELEMENTS

Premise 1
1. Parents can provide goods that non-parents cannot provide, such as earnest praise, joy, and familial identification; plus bonding, imprinting, and so on.
2. These goods require large quantities of high-quality time.
3. These goods cannot be dispensed in small quantities of time.
4. There is no adequate substitute for these goods.

Premise 8
1. Nurturing is the most important good that can be provided; it develops the essential character of children.
2. In its best form nurturing is: 1 through 4 above.
3. Material goods do not develop the essential character of children.

case if the elements are not of equal weight, and element q, for example, turns out to be one of the major questions of interest.

If we applied this rule to premises 1 and 8 we would find that most of the elements that make up premise 1 also are contained in premise 8, with the addition that premise 8 contains additional elements. Thus, premise 8 would be the most appropriate premise to evaluate, as can be seen in Table Eight. Since premise 8 contains everything in premise 1, plus more, it becomes the choice for an evaluation.

The execution of this method is relative to the practitioner. One critic may see more or less in certain premises. Thus, John may see more in premise 8, while Mary sees more in premise 1. This causes no difficulty because these guidelines are set down in order to aid the practitioner in making a choice of which premise to evaluate based upon how much he sees in the premise.

The whole process is summarized as follows:

Step One:	Find assertions	= premises 1, 2, 5, 6, and 8
Step Two:	Find crucial prem-ises	= premise 2 depends upon premise 1
		premise 5 depends upon premise 6
		premises 1, 6, and 8 are crucial premises
Step Three:	Judge controversial premises	= premise 6 is not controversial
		premise 1 has four items (see Table Eight)
		premise 8 has all items in premise 1 plus two more
		premise 8 is the most controversial and should be the focus of evaluation

There are times when one will want to evaluate a premise justified as a "fact." The reason for this is that one is disputing a generally agreed-upon piece of information. It is important that this dispute lead to a disagreement on the thrust of the author's position; otherwise, it would be a distinction without a difference.

In the sample there is only one premise justified as a fact, premise 4. This "fact" is based upon the idea that full-time outside careers require forty hours per week. However, it might be possible to spend fourteen hours per day at home; sleep four hours a night, and still have forty hours to spread over seven days (with 8.5 minutes for commuting each way). Thus, someone might want to contradict premise 4 on the basis of the above calculation. Such a contention could prove injurious to the eventual conclusion. However, it would also have to show that large numbers of people could last on four hours of sleep, get to work in 8.5 minutes, *and* survive on a steady diet of this. Such an exercise would count as an example of disputing a fact in an evaluation.

It is also wise to observe the caution noted in the vocabulary section of Chapter Two on historical figures.

This chapter has moved us one step further on the list presented at the beginning of this chapter. In Chapter Two we showed how to: (a) make clear the assessed character of that which is being evaluated; and (b) analyze that character into its components.

In the present chapter techniques have been presented to direct attention to particular important components (c).

In Chapter Eight the final three points will be covered: (d) put forth a point of view directed through those components; (e) generate a reasoned argument for that point of view; and (f) show how one's view of the whole is affected by the positions taken on those components.

READING QUESTIONS

1. What are some of the general purposes of any evaluation?
2. How do we accomplish making the assessed character of the argument clear and then analyzing this into its components?
3. How does one direct attention to particular important components?
4. What is a crucial premise for evaluation?
5. What is a controversial premise?

CHAPTER EIGHT

Mechanics of evaluation

In this chapter we will go through the process of constructing an evaluation. This includes setting out a point of view through the components isolated in Chapter Seven; generating a reasoned argument for that point of view; and being able to show the significance of the position taken.

As mentioned earlier, there are two basic types of evaluation: the pro and the con. These support the point of contention found in the conclusion or repudiate it, respectively. Let's address these two types in reverse order. Note: Throughout this chapter we will continue to use the sample offered in Chapter Seven.

GENERAL RULES FOR EVALUATION

1. Create an outline and test it according to the method advocated in Chapter Two.
2. Decide which premises to evaluate. (Follow the procedure described in Chapter Seven and summarized on p. 61.)
3. Decide what position you will take on this point(s). Your position will be either positive or negative. Depending on which choice you make, the evaluation will be either "pro" or "con." Whichever choice is made, the resulting viewpoint will be expressed through the premise(s) selected in rule 2 above.
4. Use the lists created to judge the controversial premises (see Table Eight) to structure the resulting argument and essay.

(The next steps will vary according to whether one wishes to compose a pro or con evaluation.)

A CON EVALUATION

5. The general strategy of the con evaluation is this: If the inferences of an argument are tight and the premises are interlocking, then the justification of the truth of the conclusion depends upon each one of the premises. Destroy one premise and you have undermined the conclusion.

    Thus, the purpose of a con evaluation is to defeat one or more premise(s) of the original argument. It is by this means that one has exact objections that relate to the structure of the argument as presented in its strongest form (see the principle of fairness).

    a. Your conclusion is: The premise(s) (discussed in rule 2 above) are wrong; therefore, the conclusion, which depends upon them, must be rejected.
    b. Take your list from rule 4 above and create a supporting argument.
        i.   The list identifies the elements of the premise(s) in question. Next to these elements set out counterpropositions you believe to be correct.
        ii. When you are finished, try to combine redundant counterpropositions into groups. Assign a title to each group. The title should be in the form of a proposition.
        iii. Combine your titles into a supporting argument for your conclusion.
        iv. Finalize your argument according to the rules put forth in Chapter Two.
        v.   Make each title into a paragraph, adding classification and side comments where necessary to flesh out your essay.
        vi. Add an introductory paragraph describing: (a) the argument you wish to refute—citing the conclusion and any of the premises you feel are important to your presentation; (b) the importance of your selected premise(s) to the eventual outcome; and (c) briefly, why you believe the selected premise(s) to be wrong.
    c. Such an evaluation can be of any length. For simplicity, we will use the paragraph as the unit of development. But one could, just as easily, make the basic unit a multi-paragraph section or a chapter. However, when the basic units become larger, item b., i. through iii., should be expanded, accordingly.

Applying Sample Argument to Con Evaluation

Use the list created for controversial premises (see Table Eight).

COUNTERPROPOSITIONS

1. Non-parents can provide goods such as instruction and play; these are all a growing child needs.
2. Parental-only-goods can be dispersed in short intervals of time, fully consistent with a full-time outside career.
3. Even if these goods cannot be given in short intervals, the human animal is basically dependent on nature, not nurture.
4. Cultural stimulation takes money. This is as important as basic food and so forth.

5. In our materialistic society a child reared without a fundamental materialism may not be able to compete adequately when an adult.

Combine items 1 and 3, and 4 and 5.

NEW LIST

1. Non-parents can provide goods such as instruction and play; these are all a growing child needs since the rest is genetically programmed and beyond environmental effect.
2. Parental-only-goods can be dispersed in short intervals of time, fully consistent with a full time outside career.
3. Materialism is necessary both because giving your child a cultural environment takes money, and because we live in a materialistic society and the sooner the child can get used to it the better he or she will be able to survive it.

TITLES

1. Non-parents nurture just as well as parents.
2. Anything the parent needs to give can be given quickly.
3. Materialism is not all that bad.

ARGUMENT FROM TITLES

1. Non-parents nurture just as well as parents. (*assertion*)
2. Anything the parent needs to give can be given quickly. (*assertion*)
3. Both parents can be absent from their children to pursue careers without bad effects. (*1, 2*)
4. Materialism is not all that bad. (*assertion*)
5. [Two working parents can provide a materialistic environment. (*fact*)]
6. [Whatever you can provide for your children which is, on balance, positive should be provided. (*assertion*)]
7. Both parents should pursue careers outside the home. (*3 through 6*)

Sample of a Con Essay

The author of the sample argument believes that at least one parent should remain home with developing children. He bases this conclusion on an argument that has as its foundation an objectional premise which states that beyond the minimum of material goods, nurturing is more important than greater amounts of material goods. This premise is necessary for the author's conclusion. It will be the contention of this essay that such a premise is flawed because: (a) non-parents nurture just as well as parents; (b) anything the parent needs to give can be given quickly; and (c) materialism is not all that bad. Thus, this essay rejects the sample argument's key premise and the argument in which it plays an integral part.

The first point to be examined is that non-parents nurture as well as parents. This is true because the basic childhood goods are instruction and play. Instruction can be provided by anyone. All that is requisite is that the care giver possess certain educational skills. In fact, a trained instructor may be able to do a *better* job than the parent. Professional educators know the latest techniques for equipping our children with what they need to know in order to face the world. It is foolish to believe that only a parent can teach. Our entire system of public education belies such foolishness.

Also, consider the issue of play: Children need other children in order to develop those social skills so necessary for success later in life. What better place is there than the friendly confines of a day care center where your child will never be at a loss for playmates. Here, there are expensive equipment and toys that most people cannot afford or do not have the space to keep. The day care center is a new, modern way to play. It is protected from child molesters who might snatch the unfortunate child who otherwise might be forced to play in an unprotected backyard.

These two goods, play and instruction, are all a child needs environmentally. All other necessary factors are programmed genetically so that the species may survive. Children are more resilient than we realize. Look at how they have survived unscathed in much tougher eras. Why pamper them now with unnecessary affection and attention at the expense of career fulfillment? Children have most of what they need to develop right inside their genes!

*   *   *

The rest of the essay would follow in the same manner.

A PRO EVALUATION

6. The general strategy of the pro evaluation is this: You want to defend your author from the strongest attacks which could be made against the weakest or most controversial point. In this way you have helped the author where most needed.

    a. Your conclusion is: Though some may find fault with certain premises (described in rule 2 above), you believe that these objections are mistaken, and the premise(s) stands.

    b. Take your list from rule 4 and create a supporting argument.

        i.   The list identifies the elements of the premise(s) in question. Next to these elements set out possible counterpropositions that others may bring against your author. Make sure you bring up the strongest possible counterproposal. You do your author no service in defeating weak arguments.

        ii. Set out your replies to the counterarguments.

        iii. Combine and title both the counterarguments and your responses.

        iv. Finalize your arguments according to the rules found in Chapter Two.

        v.   Make each title into a paragraph, adding classification and side comments where necessary to flesh out the essay.

        vi. Create an introductory paragraph describing: (a) the argument; (b) the importance of your selected premise(s) to the proper argument; and (c) a brief overview of what you plan to do—bring up searching difficulties and then solve them.

    c. As in the "con" evaluation, pro evaluations may be of any length.

    d. It should be obvious that the pro argument is more difficult to construct than the con. The pro contains the basic parts of the con, plus it adds a further layer of argumentation (in other words, it contains a refutation of a refutation).

Applying Sample Argument to Pro Evaluation

For simplicity, let us assume that the steps in the con section represent the strongest arguments against the weakest or most controversial premise(s). Thus, we will skip these steps and refer the reader to these steps in the preceding section.

REFUTATION OF COUNTERARGUMENT

1. There is more to education than coldly dispensing facts—especially in young children up to age four. Feedback and presentation from a loved one are especially important.
2. Pre-school education involves principles of life. These are too important to leave to a stranger.
3. Too much contact with other children for an extended time breeds added disease and can undermine fragile self-development (creating a peer-dependent personality).
4. While some children *may* be more subject to nature than to nurture, many children are just the opposite! And there is no positive way to tell which way your child is until it is too late.
5. Cultural stimulation comes from the mind and not the pocketbook. It is better to have a thousand hours of a parent's time than a thousand dollars worth of toys.
6. Materialism corrupts the soul. Anything we can do to keep it away from our children is good.

TITLES AND COMBINATION

1. The parent is the best educator for pre-school children.
2. Health drawbacks are associated with day care.
3. Environment is sometimes a crucial element.
4. Culture comes from the soul and not from the pocketbook.

ARGUMENT FROM TITLES

1. The parent is the best educator for pre-school children. (*assertion*)
2. Health drawbacks are associated with day care. (*assertion*)
3. [We should always do what is best for our children. (*assertion*)]
4. We should avoid day care and have one parent nurturing pre-schoolers. (*1 through 3*)
5. Environment is sometimes a crucial element. (*assertion*)
6. Culture comes from the soul and not from the pocketbook. (*assertion*)
7. [The parent is best able to provide an environment that touches and develops the soul. (*assertion*)]
8. The parent should provide the basic environment for the child. (*5 through 7*)
9. At least one parent should remain home with pre-schoolers. (*4, 8*)

Sample of Pro Essay

The author of the sample argument believes that at least one parent should remain home with developing children. He bases this conclusion upon an argument that has as its basis a pivotal premise which states that beyond the minimum of material goods, nurturing is more important than more material goods. This premise is necessary to the author's conclusion and it is here that detractors are likely to concentrate. This essay will examine two possible objections to this thesis and then show why these objections are mistaken.

The first objection might be . . . [see con essay sample for next few paragraphs].

These objections are challenging. If correct, they destroy the author's thesis. Therefore, it is necessary to carefully explore these issues in order to decide which is correct.

First, early childhood education is not to be compared with grammar and secondary school, because the subject matter is much different. What young children are learning are not primary scholastic skills, but lessons of life and character. Which of us would voluntarily assign this task to another?

Further, such education relies heavily on personal one-to-one feedback and presentation as the child thrives on the genuine, enthusiastic, loving responses that only a parent can provide. This growth period is unique. Cold, professional dispensing of curriculum is just what the child of this age doesn't need. For these reasons it seems clear that the parent is the best educator of the pre-school child.

*   *   *

The rest of the essay would follow in the same manner.

FINAL REMARKS

The pro and con evaluations are essential tools for anyone encountering argument. These processes enable us to respond intelligently to the mass of argument which constantly confronts us.

Such decisive responses are the culmination of a long process that begins with logical outlining. At first, such a process will be laborious and slow. But as one practices the steps, they become easier to perform and many of them can be done in your head.

You will be surprised at how quickly mastery is achieved and even suppressed premises are handled adeptly. It is at this point that you will sense the power of logical argument. The capacity was there all the time; all you had to do was develop it.

READING QUESTIONS

1. What are the general rules for an evaluation?
2. What is the strategy for a "con" evaluation?
3. What is the strategy for a "pro" evaluation?
4. What are some of the steps that can be used to create a logical essay?

EXERCISES

Take the outlines you created in Chapter Six and apply the methods advocated in Chapters Seven and Eight to construct reasoned evaluations. Practice creating both "pro" and "con" evaluations. Though the con evaluations are easier, it is important that you become skillful at both.

In lieu of using the material in Chapter Six, your teacher may direct you to practice on the subject matter for your class. This will allow you to use this text as an ongoing support to supplement any current course of instruction.

CHAPTER NINE

Logical fallacy

This chapter is placed immediately after the mechanics of evaluation because recognizing and responding to logical fallacy is a large part of evaluation. Most books on persuasion contain some catalogue of logical fallacies. However, there is no agreement upon which fallacies ought to be introduced or upon how to group them—even the exact definition of a particular fallacy may vary from text to text. There is no unanimity.

That aside, several things can be said about logical fallacies. First, a logical fallacy is an argument. As an argument it can be outlined. Second, logical fallacies *are* powerful persuaders. They shouldn't be, but they are. These arguments should not persuade, because they are bad arguments. But what makes them bad? Several answers can be given, but for the purposes of this text we will consider the content of the argument as the chief cause.* Our classification will follow accordingly.

Logical fallacy is quite prevalent. Many arguments that one encounters are logical fallacies. These are evaluated in the same general manner as described in Chapters Seven and Eight, however; care must be taken to recognize these forms of persuasion for what they are: pretenders to legitimate argument.

Much can be and has been written on logical fallacy.** My purpose here is to provide a mere glimpse of the operation of this pretender. What will be presented is enough to prepare the student for encountering this all-too-frequent form of persuasion in order that he or she may be able to combat it through an appropriate evaluation.

* Other causes require the machinery of formal logic for their presentation.
** A few of the more famous of these are noted at the end of this chapter.

Like logical argument, logical fallacy seeks to persuade. The problem is that its means are not legitimate. It uses tricks and sleights of hand to distract and confuse while the audience is being manipulated. To be manipulated by another is to become that person's slave. None of us would prefer to be slaves.

Thus, a few remarks on the types of fallacies and how to uncover them with an outline are instructive.

SHIFTING THE GROUNDS

This first classification of logical fallacy has to do with rearranging the grounds of the premises. A case is assembled in the premises which is not directly relevant to the conclusion.

The first two fallacies will be illustrated by a common situation. Let us assume for our sample a situation in which the Allied Commanders in World War II were discussing the invasion of Normandy.

In the interests of historical accuracy we will not identify the interlocutors such as General George Marshall or General Alan Brooke. Rather, we will just say General A, General B, and so on.

Argument against the Speaker (*argumentum ad hominem*)

EXAMPLE ONE

GENERAL A: I think an invasion of France near Bayeux might be a good idea. It would afford the least resistance and militarily would be the most defensible.

GENERAL B: You Yankees don't know anything about it. You're from across the Atlantic. Besides, you're always hot for hairbrained schemes—it's that gambling blood inherited from all those cowboys of yours.

Comment: General B has not offered a proper logical evaluation of General A's argument. Instead, General B has tried to shift the grounds of the argument away from General A's plan to the General himself. Unless a person's character or circumstances are functionally relevant to the argument at hand, they should not be raised. This can readily be seen when we try to outline General B's argument.

1. To know geographic facts relevant to a military operation requires one to have lived near the site in question. (*assertion*)
2. General A has not lived near France. (*fact*)
3. General A should not opine about a military operation in France. (*1, 2*)
4. A person's ability to make a rational decision is dependent on the clear thinking of all that nation's people. (*assertion*)
5. Some American cowboys were not clear thinkers. (*fact*)

6.   No American should be trusted to make a rational decision. (*4, 5*)

7.   No American should consult on a European invasion. (*3, 6*)

When set out in this way the stupidity of premises 1 and 4 becomes clear. But often this form of fallacy is persuasive. An audience can quickly forget the topic at hand when an attack is begun against the speaker. It is perhaps for this reason that *argumentum ad hominem* is a favorite among politicians.

Argument by Coercion (*argumentum ad baculum*)

EXAMPLE TWO

GENERAL A: If you don't think our plan is the right way to invade the continent, remember we can take our support elsewhere. And without our support, you'll be invaded in a week.

Comment: This argument contains a fallacy. It becomes apparent after outlining.

1.   Above all else, Britain does not want to be conquered by the Nazis. (*assertion*)
2.   At the time of speaking the only thing stopping the Nazi invasion is the presence of U.S. forces in England. (*assertion*)
3.   U.S. presence is contingent upon Britain accepting the American's D-Day proposal as the best plan. (*assertion*)
4.   Britain will accept the U.S. D-Day proposal as the best plan. (*1 through 3*)

From the outline it is clear that Britain's acceptance of the D-Day proposal as the best plan comes *not* from the proposal's military merits, but from the U.S.'s threat. The grounds of argument have been shifted to a point of power leverage. This "blackmail" is common to the various forms of *argumentum ad baculum*. It is not a logical form of persuasion. It depends upon the idea that "might makes right."

Similarly, the other fallacies that involve shifting the grounds of argument may be outlined and found logically to be irrelevant to the stated point of contention. The reader is invited to construct his own outline to prove this.

Below are brief descriptions of other logical fallacies that fit under the general classification of shifting grounds.

Argument from Ignorance

This fallacy rests on the notion that a proposition is true simply because it has never been proven false, and vice versa.

EXAMPLE THREE

No one conclusively has proven ESP false. Therefore, it must be true.

Comment: Just because there have been no successful proofs that ESP is false does not demonstrate that it *cannot* be proven false. Maybe we have not been inventive enough in our examinations of ESP. The premise only shows that it is still an open question.

Appeal to Pity

The vehicle of persuasion here is emotion. The functional facts are disregarded in favor of overpowering sentiment. Thus, a lawyer or senator may make his case on the basis of some irrelevant plea.

EXAMPLE FOUR

You should not convict my client because he has led a difficult life full of disappointment,

or

We should save the Heritage Clock Company because it has been a part of all of our lives since we were children. How can we allow a fixture of our past to go under?

Comment: Neither of these arguments addresses the facts. They depend upon such specious, suppressed premises as "whoever has many disappointments may be excused from living according to the law," or "all fond institutional fixtures of our past should be preserved." When outlined with all the requisite premises, these illogical premises become obvious. Those who do not engage in outlining may very well find themselves hoodwinked by this powerful mode of persuasion.

Social Identification

This is one of the most frequently used forms in advertising. It is sometimes called "keeping up with the Jones's." If the persuader can convince you that "everyone" is doing something, then the reader is drawn to conforming. Perhaps this natural tendency comes from some deep biological origin rooted in our being social animals. But this, of course, says nothing about what logically ought to be the case.

One can include in this type of fallacy all nonlogical identifications based on a "me-too" principle. An example might be the association of a product with a well-dressed model in front of a Rolls-Royce. Yet, no one would agree with the premise that "anyone who purchases product *x* will drive a Rolls and be successful and happy." It is ludicrous when stated as such.

Still, this fallacy is based on some social identification akin to this. The source of this feeling is similar to one everyone knows: When the entire room rises to give a standing ovation, it is difficult to resist joining in—even if you don't agree that the performance deserved it. Social identification is one of the most powerful primitive forces that influences human behavior. Since it is so powerful, it is even more important to try to outline such forms and expose this sort of fallacy when it occurs.

Authority

There are two forms of this fallacy: disconnected and connected.

Disconnected authority refers to authorities in one area being used to support a position or product in an area foreign to their expertise. Thus, a baseball player may be used to promote a breakfast cereal—or a rock star may be used to support a political cause. In each case, the force of persuasion is that someone who knows something about one area will know something about all areas. This is obviously false. One's respect for an authority's expertise is not logically transferable.

Connected authority occurs when one accepts a point of contention *merely* because an authority says so. Even if the source is an expert in that field, one should not accept a conclusion *just* because an authority asserts it. For example, Mr. Smith may be an expert in ethics, but one should not accept his judgment that abortion is moral or immoral *just* because he says so. What is required is an argument along with it. It is the *argument* that should persuade, not merely an authority.

Now it is true that not every point can be traced to its origins. Sometimes we must accept certain points without thorough analysis. In these cases connected authority is generally more reliable than unconnected authority or no authority, but it should always be accepted that the use of an authority creates a contingent chain that is open to question. The longer the chain, the greater the possibility for error. This caveat should always be kept in mind when using argument from connected authority.

Begging the Question

One effective way to shift the grounds of the argument is to beg the question. Traditionally, this has been defined as assuming what you are trying to prove.

EXAMPLE FIVE

Opium produces sleep because of its dormitive powers. (Molière poking fun at Aristotelian science.)

Comment: What is at question is *why* opium causes people to sleep. But the reason given is that opium has sleep-producing powers. This is precisely what is at issue. The point of contention is not proven by the premises. Thus, begging the question is an illegitimate type of argument.

What tips one off to begging the question is the presence of premises which, instead of causing the conclusion, actually depend upon the conclusion for their own veracity.

Beware of premises which seem to be merely a restatement of the conclusion.

Changing the Question

In this form you shift the grounds of the argument away from the issue under discussion and to another issue which you can answer. For example, if someone asked a vice-president for marketing why sales were down, the vice-president might reply by detailing the advertising campaign used in the past year. The question was not about the ad campaign, but about the dip in revenue. Thus, the grounds for the argument have been shifted.

The shift in attention can occur in the premises or in the conclusion itself. When it occurs in the premises the speaker "re-defines" the question into an entirely different issue (as in the above case).

When the change occurs in the conclusion, the conclusion does not follow from the premises. (This is often called irrelevant conclusion.)

EXAMPLE SIX

STUDENT: You can't flunk me, Ms. Hightower.
Ms. HIGHTOWER: Why not? You flunked all your assignments.
STUDENT: You can't flunk me because I need a good grade to stay on the volleyball team. Besides, I really liked your class.

Comment: The premises in this case have nothing to do with the conclusion. The student has changed the question from *what he deserves* to *what would be convenient.*

Often someone employing this type of argument fallacy rambles on and on, hoping the audience will forget the original point of contention. Then he draws his conclusion. But upon outlining such an argument it will be found that the inferences are loose and the premises do not interlock. Outlining will make the shift apparent.

Dilemma Question

This fallacy focuses attention away from the principal issue by offering a false choice. Because the choice appears to be exhaustive, it makes an insinuation which it has no business making.

A classic example is the old joke: "Have you stopped beating your wife yet?" Either answer of "yes" or "no" is misleading. The same is true of the slogan, "Would you rather be dead or Red?" There is no logical reason why these are the real alternatives.

For example, there might be a Senate debate about sending U.S. troops to some foreign country to stop communism. An advocate of the deployment might ask an opponent, "Would you rather be Red or are you willing to fight for your freedom?" The implication is that unless troops are deployed, the country in question—and eventually the United States—will fall to communism. This shifts the emphasis away from whether this particular deployment is prudent and will, in fact, do what it is claimed it will do.

The focus of the argument should be on the *means* of attaining the objective that all would agree upon. However, the argument is shifted away from that focus and onto the goals themselves. The means are assumed and linked to general goals to which all agree. It does this by creating a false dilemma. The attention of the argument is focused away from where it should be.

The last three fallacies in this section primarily have to do with inductive argument. The reader is encouraged to refresh his memory of this type of argument by reviewing the presentation of induction in Chapter Three.

Hasty Generalization

This fallacy comes about when a generalization is formed from an atypical sample. Instead of properly following the rules of induction, the author considers the cases improperly. The practitioner of this fallacy can be said to "jump to conclusions."

Three of the most common reasons for doing so are: (a) the sample isn't large enough; (b) the sample isn't varied enough; and (c) the practitioner has been psychologically swayed.

EXAMPLE SEVEN

Mr. Johnson concluded that Mrs. Smith would win the election for U.S. Senator because most of his friends favored Mrs. Smith.

Comment: In this case, Mr. Johnson formed a generalization based upon an atypical sample; the sample is too small and it is not varied enough. Thus, the conclusions may not be correct.

There are, of course, times when a small sample causes no difficulty. If someone wanted to test the boiling point of water or the melting point of lead, a large number of tests would be unnecessary. For more on the correct procedure of induction, see Chapter Three.

Sometimes a person may be swayed even though the facts point otherwise. For example, Joan might acquire all the relevant information on buying a station wagon. As a result, she decides that the DeSoto wagon is the best. But later she demurs when a friend at work tells her that the DeSoto wagon *he* bought turned out to be a lemon. In this case Joan allows herself to be swayed from a sound judgment by the immediacy of the situation—a situation which represents an atypical case.

Improper Analogy

This fallacy results from improperly shifting grounds from properties belonging to one statement to those of another. Generally, the former is well known and the description beyond dispute. The latter is controversial. The use of the analogy represents an attempt to fix the character of the latter.

For example, one might properly agree to the saying, "Where there's smoke, there's fire." This is generally a true statement. But even if one agrees to the saying, he or she might disagree with various applications of this, such as indicating that wrongdoing has occurred whenever there is a climate of negative innuendo.

Another example can be found in Plato's *Crito*. Socrates defended his accepting the state's punishment partly because he likened the state to his father. The reader in such an instance must decide whether analogy is fulfilling its proper role or is merely acting as a figure of speech to illustrate the author's point—which has no real logical content.

Incomplete Evidence

Often, we must make judgments without having all the possible evidence before us. This is a practical necessity. But sometimes this can lead us into error.

EXAMPLE EIGHT

The President of the United States is not listed in the Washington, D.C. phone directory. Therefore, he must not have a private phone.

Comment: The Washington, D.C. phone directory is quite comprehensive, but it does not list the phone number of every private telephone. Some are unlisted. The inference in Example Eight is based upon incomplete evidence.

SHIFTING THE TERMS

In this second classification of logical fallacy the focus is on shifting the terms themselves in various ways so that what appears to be a tight inference really is not. It is an illusion created by *ambiguity* and by *false inference*. Each of these divisions, in turn, has three subclasses. As with shifting grounds, the best defense is to set out a clear outline and examine it closely.

Ambiguity

A. *Equivocation* creates ambiguity by using one term and assigning two different meanings to the term.

EXAMPLE ONE

1. Madmen should be put in a nuthouse. (*assertion*)
2. My father often gets mad. (*fact*)
3. My father should be put in a nuthouse. (*1, 2*)

1. Reagan controls a ballooning budget. (*assertion*)
2. Balloons are controlled by hot air. (*fact*)
3. Reagan is a bunch of hot air. (*1, 2*)

Comment: These arguments are not logically valid because in the first case the word 'mad' is used in two senses. There is no logical connection between the two premises because there are no common terms by which an inference may be drawn.

The same is true of the two senses of 'balloon' in the second case. Logical inference requires some common ground by which it may create a new proposition. ("Mediate" inference requires at least two premises; "immediate" inference requires only one.) In the above examples this appears to be the case, but upon examination of the logical outline, it is seen not to be.

In equivocation, ambiguity is created since multiple meanings legitimately exist. Unless the exact same meaning is maintained throughout, illogical conclusions may be drawn. To guard against possible equivocation, try substituting synonyms for the disputed terms and then test for validity.

B. *Amphiboly* creates two distinct meanings from a poorly formed grammatical structure.

EXAMPLE TWO

Those who ice fish often catch colds.
The stockbroker killed himself after an affectionate farewell from his fiancée with a shotgun.

Comment: In the first example it is unclear whether the word 'often' attaches to "ice fish" or to "catch colds." The sentence's meaning is different in the two cases.

The second sample is likewise caught between the two meanings implied by the dangling phrase "with a shotgun." The effect is that the dangling phrase may attach to the manner of the stockbroker's death *or* to the manner of his affectionate farewell.

Though these above examples seem comic, the amphiboly can cause very serious effects. Documents released from World War II suggest that the Japanese sent a message that was an invitation to discuss surrender *before* our dropping of the atomic bomb. The message was misread due to amphiboly. Think how history has been changed due to this single instance of logical fallacy!

Proper grammatical structuring should alleviate this difficulty. When reformulating another's argument and two possibilities obtain, one should, by the principle of fairness, always choose the stronger interpretation.

C. *Accent* owes its multiple meanings to an unusual context. The sentence as literally read has one meaning and the context creates another, unstated meaning. For example, if you wrote on an employee's work report, "Harris was sober today," you would not literally be saying anything harmful. But the context seems to emphasize that though Harris was sober today, on other days he is not.

Quoting out of context, or other alterations of the context, may create this fallacy. The way to uncover this difficulty is to outline it and supply the proper context as background conditions (perhaps via suppressed premises).

False Inferences

A. *False cause* occurs when there is no good evidence by which to infer a causal relationship. This may be the most dangerous of all the groups of fallacies, because it may appear to many to represent a proper inference. Part of the reason for this is that often one cannot isolate a general methodology that dictates that it is always the case that such and such exercise of it is wrong. Compare these two instances from the following example:

EXAMPLE THREE

More students go to college today than in 1915, and the country is filled with more violence today than in 1915. Therefore, sending young people to college causes a rise in violence.

Of all cocaine addicts, 98 percent started out drinking coffee before their drug use, and later they moved to cocaine. Therefore, drinking coffee leads to cocaine addiction.

Comment: These two selections operate on different principles. In the first selection the conclusion is justified by *post hoc ergo propter hoc*. This is an improper justification. Just because something happens after something else does not mean that a causal relationship has been established. Yet the standard definition of cause as the constant conjunction of temporally contiguous events seems, structurally, to be very similar to the fallacy.

What is needed is *more* than knowing that one group of actions followed another group to assert causation. More cases need to be examined to determine whether or not a constant conjunction occurs. Such research would require all the controls of modern scientific method. Yet, even at that there will be controversial cases such as the alleged cause and effect relationship between pornography and sexual violence.

In the second example, statistical correlation is the vehicle of inference. As with the first example, there are proper and improper usages of this principle. It was statistical correlation which established the link between cigarette smoking and cancer. This was a valid implementation of the technique, but it is obvious that such a method can easily be abused.

The best way to steer clear of failures from either of the above modes is to endeavor to connect the usage in question to some body of established scientific theory. Such a strategy is called "projection." It dictates that one be able to project the unknown or disputed causal relationship into an entrenched paradigm. This amounts to finding the mechanisms and placing those mechanisms into an accepted common body of knowledge.

In most cases such a projection works. However, when whole bodies of scientific knowledge change it is useless. But these cases are rare. In general, careful scrutiny and projection are one's best tools against false cause.

B. *Composition* is less intricate. This fallacy states that properties properly assigned to the *part* may also be assigned to the *whole*. For example, one could have very sturdy bricks (parts) and yet construct a very flimsy building (whole) with those bricks. In this case the whole has a different property than the individual parts have when they are examined separately.

C. *Division* is just the opposite of composition. This fallacy states that properties properly assigned to the *whole* may also be assigned to the *part*.

EXAMPLE FOUR

1. The Federal bureaucracy is inefficient. (*assertion*)
2. Joe works in the Federal bureaucracy. (*fact*)
3. Joe is inefficient. (*1, 2*)

1. Lions are virtually extinct. (*fact*)
2. Simba is a young lion. (*fact*)
3. Simba is virtually extinct. (*1, 2*)

Comment: These examples both demonstrate that the individual does not necessarily share in the properties of the whole. It is perfectly coherent to have a very efficient Joe and a very healthy Simba. The whole and its properties may be of a different level of logical description than that of the part. This is because the class is a different logical type than the individual. When we ascribe properties to the class we do so in a different way than when we ascribe properties to an individual—for example, no one would claim the *class* of red-headed men to be red headed.

Untangling this relationship is too intricate for our present purpose and is an issue of dispute among philosophers of language. However, it is clear that in general the fallacy of division occurs when we examine non-essential traits and distribute them to each member. Thus, Joe is not a part of the Federal bureaucracy by virtue of his being efficient or inefficient. The defining characteristic has to do with who pays his salary. Therefore, inefficiency is an accident and does not necessarily distribute among the members of the class. Likewise, being extinct is an accidental property of lions. Therefore, no necessary link can be made to one of the parts.

Much of this analysis applies to composition as well, except that in the case of the fallacy of composition we are talking about a synonymy between the essential traits of the parts and those of the whole. Where there is no synonymy, or when the traits are accidental and not essential, the fallacy of composition may result.

Failures to distinguish these differences can lead to false inferences. Throughout, the student should familiarize himself with logical fallacies as aides for creating correct evaluations.

FURTHER READING

ARISTOTLE, *Sophistical Refutations*.

H. W. B. JOSEPH, *An Introduction to Logic* (London: Oxford University Press, 1906).

W. WARD FEARNSIDE and WILLIAM B. HOLTHER, *Fallacy: The Counterfeit of Argument* (Englewood Cliffs, N.J.: Prentice-Hall, 1959).

DAVID HACKETT FISCHER, *Historian's Fallacies* (New York: Harper and Row, 1970).

C. L. HAMBLIN, *Fallacies* (London: Methuen, 1970).

EDWARD T. DAMER, *Attacking Faulty Reasoning* (Belmont, Calif.: Wadsworth, 1980).

IRVING M. COPI, *Introduction to Logic*, 6th ed. (New York: Macmillan, 1982).

READING QUESTIONS

Directions: Below are two exercise groups. For each exercise indicate which fallacy is being committed. Be prepared to create a logical outline to justify your judgment and to show how the fallacy operates.

GROUP A

1. Chairman of the Board: Before I ask for a vote on the correctness of my vision for our company's future, let me remind you that I have the power to fire any one of you anytime I want. Now, who thinks my report does not describe the best path to the future?
    Nobody dissents.

2. Like as the waves make towards the pebbled shore,
    So do our minutes hasten to their end.

    —Shakespeare

3. Daddy Bigbucks: The way to get my baseball team into the World Series is to buy the best players I can for each position.

4. Reginald: Who's coming to dinner tomorrow, dear?
    Lady B: No one you'd know. Freddy Goodfellow, an architect, and Lady Highbirth.
    Reginald: Does that make two or three?

5. Travel Guide: The Swani are not a mobile people. Suitcases are seldom found.
   Lady B: Oh, Reggie, if that's true we must be certain not to lose sight of ours!

6. Most painters are not scientists. Therefore, Leonardo da Vinci was not a scientist.

7. Professor Plum: Homer was a greater poet than Wolfgang Wieland.
   Miss Scarlet: Why?
   Plum: Because all the critics agree this is so.
   Scarlet: Why do they agree?
   Plum: Because Homer's a greater poet.

8. People have been talking for years about a bill to reform the Electoral College. Most of these arguments have real merit. The Electoral College is undemocratic and is contrary to the basic ideals of our nation. However, I don't think such a bill will ever pass.

9. Our country is at a crossroad: Either we cut domestic spending or we face an unmanageable national debt.

10. One of the advancements of twentieth-century painting is that imitating nature is no longer a goal. Thus, imitation is a discarded notion for artists.

11. IBM is the best computing company in the world. I am a systems analyst for IBM. I am therefore one of the best systems analysts in the world.

12. Most philosophers are male. Therefore, Margaret Green, a philosopher, is a male.

13. Fine cooking is an art. The repository for art is an art museum. Thus, fine cooking should be displayed in art museums.

14. Drinking whiskey is evil because it is the Devil's brew, and anything connected to the Devil is evil.

15. Who is the best novelist in America? There are many responses one could make here. However, one important issue is who turns in his manuscripts on time. Every editor prefers an author who meets his deadlines. One author I've worked with who fits this description is Angus Black. This man is *always* on time and frequently early. Really. No bull.

16. What should we do in the United States: put drug pushers into the gas chamber, or let the moral fabric of our country decay?

17. Don't ask Sue's opinion about whether it's hard work. She's from Southern California, and we all know what their idea of a day's work is.

18. No one has proven that Sharkey has committed the murder. Therefore, he's innocent.

19. How can we ever turn immigrants away from our country? These are the tired, the poor, the huddled masses yearning to be free. We are their last hope! Can we say, "No"?

20. Buy America's best-selling film—Kodak.

21. Use the gasoline baseball pitcher Tom Seaver uses—Exxon.

22. Author: The review of my book says it's an excellent example of a boring, trite, muddled detective novel.
    Editor: Let's just say, "An excellent . . . . detective novel." That will look good on the dust jacket.

23. No mathematician has ever proven the truth of Goldbach's Conjecture. Thus, it must be false.

24. Shave with the razor John McEnroe uses—Bic.

25. Father: Now, Suzy, I'll have no more of your complaining tonight.
    Suzy: All right. I'll just complain the same amount as last night.

26. Ronald Reagan, a former actor, says that Paul Newman is the best active film actor. Therefore, it must be true.

27. Everytime I've ever washed my car it rained later in the day and undid my work. Therefore, I'll stop washing my car. Who wants to put in all that trouble for nothing?

28. Al Lopez, a former Big League manager, said the designated hitter rule is a poor one. Clearly, it should be eliminated.

29. Lady B: I never accept social engagements on nights which are under a full moon. You never know what will happen. All the crazies are brought out.

30. Buddy Crocker: Just think what a fine meal someone could have if he were served all the winning dishes from this year's National Cooking Contest!

31. The Midwest is a geologically flat region. Mt. Rushmore is in the Midwest, so Mt. Rushmore is flat.

32. 'Tis education forms the common mind,
    Just as the twig is bent, the tree's inclined.

    —Alexander Pope

33. Why listen to the Supreme Court Justices? They're too old to know anything, anyway.

GROUP B*

1. ANTIPHOLUS E.:   Go fetch me something; I'll break open the gate.
   DROMIO S: (from within)   Break any breaking here, and I'll break your knave's pate.
   DROMIO E.:   A man may break a word with you sir, and words are but wind:
   Ay, and break it in your face, so he break it not behind.
   DROMIO S: (from within)   It seems thou want'st breaking. Out upon thee, hind!
   DROMIO E.:   Here's too much 'Out upon thee!' I pray thee, let me in.
   DROMIO S: (from within)   Ay, when fowls have no feathers, and fish have no fin.
   ANTIPHOLUS E.:   Well, I'll break in. Go borrow me a crow.
   DROMIO E.:   A crow without feather? Master, mean you so?
   For a fish without a fin, there's a fowl without a feather:
   If a crow help us in, sirrah, we'll pluck a crow together.
   ANTIPHOLUS E.:   Go thee gone; fetch me an iron crow.
   —Shakespeare, *A Comedy of Errors*

2. "There are general laws current in the world as to morality, 'Thou shalt not steal,' for instance. That has necessarily been current as a law through all nations. But the first man you meet in the street will have ideas about theft so different from yours, that if you knew them as you know your own, you would say that this law and yours were not even founded on the same principle. It is compatible with this man's honesty to cheat you in a matter of horseflesh; with that man's in a traffic of railway shares; with that other man's as to a woman's fortune; with a fourth's anything may be done for a seat in

---

* Note on words: knave = servant; pate = head; hind = servant; crow = (a) a type of bird; (b) a crow bar used for prying things open; and (c) to pluck a crow is a settling of accounts; sirrah = fellow (a contemptuous form of address).

Parliament; while the fifth man, who stands high among us, and who implores his God every Sunday to write that law on his heart, spends every hour of his daily toil in a system of fraud, and is regarded as a 'pattern of national commerce'!"

—Anthony Trollope, *Phineas Finn*

3. "Mr Pinch's the most hideous, goggle-eyed creature in existence," resumed Merry, "quite an ogre. The ugliest, awkwardest, frightfullest being you can imagine. This is his syster, so I leave you to suppose what *she* is. I shall be obliged to laught outright, I know I shall!"

—Charles Dickens, *Martin Chuzzlewit*

4. "The thing is . . . . she told Agatha Runcible she wasn't *going* to ask me."
    "Why not?"
    "Apparently she's in a rage about something I said about something she said about Miles."
    "People do take things so seriously," said Adam encouragingly.
    "It means ruin for me," said Lord Balcairn. "Isn't that Pamela Popham?"
    "I haven't the least idea."
    "I'm sure it is. . . . I must look up the spelling in the stud book when I get back. I got into awful trouble about spelling the other day. . . . Ruin. . . . She's asked Vanburgh."
    "Well, he's some sort of cousin, isn't he?"
    "It's so damned unfair. All my cousins are in lunatic asylums or else they live in the country and do indelicate things with wild animals . . . except my mamma, and that's worse. . . . They were furious at the office about Van getting that Downing Street 'scoop.' If I miss this party I may as well leave Fleet Street for good . . . I may as well put my head into a gas oven and have done with it . . . I'm sure if Margot knew how much it meant to me she wouldn't mind my coming."
    Great tears stood in his eyes threatening to overflow.

—Evelyn Waugh, *Vile Bodies*

5. But if it be agreed we shall be tried by visions, there is a vision recorded by Eusebius, far ancienter than this tale of Jerome. . . . Dionysius Alexandrinus was, about the year 240, a person of great name in the church for piety and great learning, who had wont to avail himself much against heretics by being conversant in their books . . . this is confirmed [in the great man's writings]: "Read any books whatever come to thy hands, for thou art sufficient be to judge aright and to examine each matter."* To this revelation he assented the sooner as he confesses because it was answerable to that of the apostle to the Thessalonians: "Prove all things, hold fast that which is good."**
    And he might have added another remarkable saying of the same author: "To the pure, all things are pure;" not only meats and drinks, but all kind of knowledge whether of good or evil; [therefore] knowledge cannot defile, nor consequently can books if the will and conscience be not defiled.

—John Milton, *Areopagitica*

---

* Milton's loose quotation from Eusebius's *Ecclesiastical History*.

** The Epistle to the Thessalonians is a book from the Bible.

CHAPTER TEN

The big picture

The purpose of this last chapter is to fill in a few gaps by providing additional contexts in which outlines can be used to unlock the structures of various argumentative texts. As always, the general execution of this task will be suggestive rather than comprehensive.

MICRO- AND MACRO-ARGUMENTS

Throughout this primer the emphasis has been on outlining arguments that occur in several paragraphs or at most in a few pages. Such arguments are the atomic building blocks upon which larger arguments may be constructed. In this way the conclusions from small arguments become premises for larger arguments. For example, a chapter itself might have an argumentative structure. Such an argument could be outlined using the same techniques described in Chapter Two. The main difference is that the text is of greater length and the references to the premises are less explicit. For this reason the best way to prepare for outlining the macro-argument is to begin with outlines of the micro-arguments contained within it.

The larger argument emerges from the conclusions of the various micro-arguments. In this way understanding the macro-argument involves apprehending the relationship of the atomic micro-arguments. It is this larger structure that affords a deeper understanding of what an author is trying to say. One's reconstruction of the macro-argument may involve some tampering with the micro-arguments according to the principle of fairness set out in the Introduction. The parts influence our understanding of the whole and vice versa. This dynamic tension between part and whole

TABLE NINE: Macro- and Micro-Arguments

Atomic Micro-arguments	Chapter Macro-arguments	Book Macro-argument

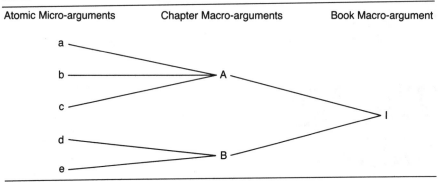

allows a fuller understanding of context in accordance with the pluralism principle set out in Chapter Seven.

Sometimes a whole book has an argument which may be reconstructed from the chapter arguments. The difference lies in the levels of generality involved. As one describes a progressively larger and larger section of text, the premises of the macro-arguments themselves come from increasingly general sections of text. These relations are pictorially depicted in Table Nine.

The same types of dynamic interaction can occur between chapter macro-arguments and book macro-arguments. This complicates the contextual fabric and thus enhances comprehension through the pluralism principle.

Examples of this level of argument are difficult to present in a slim volume such as this because of space constraints. However, some flavor for the macro-argument can be presented through an examination of the Declaration of Independence. This level of macro-argument more closely resembles the chapter-level macro-argument.

EXAMPLE ONE

THE UNANIMOUS DECLARATION OF THE THIRTEEN
UNITED STATES OF AMERICA

When in the Course of human Events, it becomes necessary for one People to dissolve the Political Bands which have connected them with another, and to assume among the Powers of the Earth, the separate and equal Station to which the Laws of Nature and of Nature's God entitle them, a decent Respect to the Opinions of Mankind requires that they should declare the causes which impel them to the Separation.

We hold these Truths to be self-evident, that all Men are created equal, that they are endowed by their Creator with certain unalienable Rights, that among these are Life, Liberty, and the Pursuit of Happiness—That to secure these Rights, Governments are instituted among Men, deriving their just

Powers from the Consent of the Governed, that whenever any Form of Government becomes destructive of these Ends, it is the Right of the People to alter or to abolish it, and to institute new Government, laying its Foundation on such Principles, and organizing its Powers in such Form, as to them shall seem most likely to effect their Safety and Happiness. Prudence, indeed, will dictate that Governments long established should not be changed for light and transient Causes; and accordingly all Experience hath shewn, that Mankind are more disposed to suffer, while Evils are sufferable, than to right themselves by abolishing the Forms to which they are accustomed. But when a long Train of Abuses and Usurpations, pursuing invariably the same Object, evinces a Design to reduce them under absolute Despotism, it is their Right, it is their Duty, to throw off such Government, and to provide new Guards for their future Security. Such has been the patient Sufferance of these Colonies; and such is now the Necessity which constrains them to alter their former Systems of Government. The History of the present King of Great-Britain is a History of repeated Injuries and Usurpations, all having in direct Object the Establishment of an absolute Tyranny over these States. To prove this, let Facts be submitted to a candid World.

He has refused his Assent to Laws, the most wholesome and necessary for the public Good.

He has forbidden his Governors to pass Laws of immediate and pressing Importance, unless suspended in their Operation till his Assent should be obtained; and when so suspended, he has utterly neglected to attend to them.

He has refused to pass other Laws for the Accommodation of large Districts of People, unless those People would relinquish the Right of Representation in the Legislature, a Right inestimable to them, and formidable to Tyrants only.

He has called together Legislative Bodies at Places unusual, uncomfortable, and distant from the Depository of their Public Records, for the sole Purpose of fatiguing them into Compliance with his Measures.

He has dissolved Representative Houses repeatedly, for opposing with manly Firmness his Invasions on the Rights of the People.

He has refused for a long Time, after such Dissolutions, to cause others to be elected; whereby the Legislative Powers, incapable of Annihilation, have returned to the People at large for their exercise; the State remaining in the mean time exposed to all the Dangers of Invasion from without, and Convulsions within.

He has endeavoured to prevent the Population of these States; for that Purpose obstructing the Laws for Naturalization of Foreigners; refusing to pass others to encourage their Migrations hither, and raising the Conditions of new Appropriations of Lands.

He has obstructed the Administration of Justice, by refusing his Assent to Laws for establishing Judiciary Powers.

He has made Judges dependent on his Will alone, for the Tenure of their Offices, and the Amount and payment of their Salaries.

He has erected a Multitude of new Offices, and sent hither Swarms of Officers to harrass our People, and eat out their Substance.

He has kept among us, in Times of Peace, Standing Armies, without the consent of our Legislatures.

He has affected to render the Military independent of, and superior to the Civil Power.

He has combined with others to subject us to a Jurisdiction foreign to our Constitution, and unacknowledged by our Laws; giving his Assent to their Acts of pretended Legislation:

For quartering large Bodies of Armed Troops among us:

For protecting them, by a mock Trial, from Punishment for any Murders which they should commit on the Inhabitants of these States:

For cutting off our Trade with all Parts of the World:

For imposing Taxes on us without our Consent:

For depriving us, in many Cases, of the Benefits of Trial by Jury:

For transporting us beyond Seas to be tried for pretended Offences:

For abolishing the free System of English Laws in a neighbouring Province, establishing therein an arbitrary Government, and enlarging its Boundaries, so as to render it at once an Example and fit Instrument for introducing the same absolute Rule into these Colonies:

For taking away our Charters, abolishing our most valuable Laws, and altering fundamentally the Forms of our Governments:

For suspending our own Legislatures, and declaring themselves invested with Power to legislate for us in all Cases whatsoever.

He has abdicated Government here, by declaring us out of his Protection and waging War against us.

He has plundered our Seas, ravaged our Coasts, burnt our towns, and destroyed the Lives of our People.

He is, at this Time, transporting large Armies of foreign Mercenaries to compleat the works of Death, Desolation, and Tyranny, already begun with circumstances of Cruelty and Perfidy, scarcely paralleled in the most barbarous Ages, and totally unworthy the Head of a civilized Nation.

He has constrained our fellow Citizens taken Captive on the high Seas to bear Arms against their Country, to become the Executioners of their Friends and Brethren, or to fall themselves by their Hands.

He has excited domestic Insurrections amongst us, and has endeavoured to bring on the Inhabitants of our Frontiers, the merciless Indian Savages, whose known Rule of Warfare, is an undistinguished Destruction, of all Ages, Sexes and Conditions.

In every stage of these Oppressions we have Petitioned for Redress in the most humble Terms: Our repeated Petitions have been answered only by repeated Injury. A Prince, whose Character is thus marked by every act which may define a Tyrant, is unfit to be the Ruler of a free People.

Nor have we been wanting in Attentions to our British Brethren. We have warned them from Time to Time of Attempts by their Legislature to extend an unwarrantable Jurisdiction over us. We have reminded them of the Circumstances of our Emigration and Settlement here. We have appealed to their native Justice and Magnanimity, and we have conjured them by the Ties of our common Kindred to disavow these Usurpations, which, would inevitably interrupt our Connections and Correspondence. They too have been deaf to the Voice of Justice and of Consanguinity. We must, therefore, acquiesce in the Necessity, which denounces our Separation, and hold them, as we hold the rest of Mankind, Enemies in War, in Peace, Friends.

We, therefore, the Representatives of the UNITED STATES OF AMERICA, in General Congress, Assembled, appealing to the Supreme Judge of the World for the Rectitude of our Intentions, do, in the Name, and by Authority of the good People of these Colonies, solemnly Publish and Declare, That these United Colonies are, and of Right ought to be, Free and Independent States; thay they are absolved from all Allegiance to the British Crown, and that all political Connection between them and the State of Great-Britain, is and ought to be totally dissolved; and that as Free and Independent States, they have full Power to levy War, conclude Peace, contract Alliances, establish Commerce, and to do all other Acts and Things which Independent States may of right do. And for the support of this declaration, with a firm Reliance on the Protection of divine Providence, we mutually pledge to each other our lives, our Fortunes, and our sacred Honor.

A few of the micro-outlines which may be constructed from this document are:

A. 1. A decent respect for mankind requires nations to declare any changes in their sovereignty. (*assertion*)
   [2. America wishes a change in its sovereignty. (*fact*)]
   [3. America has a decent respect for mankind. (*assertion*)]
   4. America will now declare its intentions for self-rule. (*1–3*)

B. 1. All humans have unalienable rights to life, liberty, and the pursuit of happiness. (*assertion*)
   2. Governments are established to protect these rights. (*assertion*)
   3. Governments are empowered by the citizens to perform their rightful tasks. (*assertion*)
   4. Governments which do not protect rights can be changed by the citizens. (*1–3*)

C. 1. There are high costs to be paid in switching governments. (*fact*)
   2. Prudence dictates choosing the lowest cost, all things being equal. (*fact*)
   3. A new government should be established only on serious grounds. (*1, 2*)

D. 1. A new government should be established only on serious grounds. (*chain argument from argument C*)
   2. A long series of abuses under despotic rule constitutes serious grounds. (*assertion*)
   3. A long series of abuses under despotic rule would permit a change in governments. (*1, 2*)
   4. The Colonies have suffered a long series of abuses under despotic rule. (*assertion*)
   5. The Colonies may change governments. (*3, 4*)

E. [1. A tyrant and despot are generally characterized by limiting their subject's self-determination and inflicting harm upon them. (*assertion.*)]
   2. The king of England has refused assent to laws, forbidden governors to pass laws, tried to abolish popular representation, obstructed the administration of justice. . . . (*fact*)
   3. The king of England has limited the colonists' self-determination. (*2*)
   4. The king of England has plundered the seas, ravaged the coasts, burnt the towns, and destroyed the lives of the colonists. (*fact*)
   5. The king of England has inflicted harm upon his subjects. (*4*)
   6. The king of England is a tyrant and a despot. (*1, 3, 5*)

F. 1. Peaceful methods of resolving political conflict refer to working through channels. (*fact*)
   2. Colonies have petitioned the crown. (*fact*)
   3. Colonies have warned the crown. (*fact*)
   4. Colonies have used moral suasion. (*fact*)
   5. Colonies have tried peaceful methods to resolve their conflict. (*1–4*)

G. 1. Tyrants and despots are unfit to rule. (*assertion*)
   [2. Every state needs a fit ruler. (*fact*)]

3. The king of England is a tyrant and a despot to the Colonies. (*chain argument from E*)
4. The king of England is unfit to rule the Colonies. (*1, 3*)
5. The Colonies need a new government. (*2, 4*)

H. 1. The colonists have tried peaceful methods to resolve their conflict. (*chain argument from F*)
2. The king of England has lent a deaf ear to their peaceful methods. (*fact*)
3. The citizens of a country have a right to self-determination. (*chain argument from B*)
4. Overthrowing the king's rule is the only way to insure self-determination. (*assertion*)
5. The American Colonies may overthrow the king of England's rule. (*1–4*)

To construct a macro-argument from these eight deductive and inductive arguments, first study the relationships between the arguments. Try to see how all the arguments might fit together into a larger argument that encompasses the general sense of the micro-arguments without going into the specific detail that they do. For example:

I. 1. Governments which do not protect rights may be changed by the citizens of that country. (*assertion from argument B*)
2. A new government should only be established as the result of very serious grounds. (*assertion from argument C*)
3. Not protecting the rights of one's citizens by a king constitutes very serious grounds. (*assertion from argument D*)
4. The king of England is a despot and a tyrant. (*assertion from argument E*)
5. Colonies may change governments. (*1–4*)
6. Every peaceful avenue should be explored in order for a people to be justified in changing governments. (*assertion from argument F*)
7. Colonies have used every peaceful avenue to address their grievances but the king has lent a deaf ear. (*fact from argument F*)
8. Colonies may employ non-peaceful means to change governments. (*6, 7*)
9. Despots are unfit to rule. (*assertion from argument G*)
10. Rulers who lend a deaf ear to legitimate complaints are unfit to rule. (*assertion from argument H*)
11. The king of England is unfit to rule. (*4, 7, 9, 10*)
12. The Colonies may change governments. (*5, 8, 11*)

Argument I takes a little something from each argument: Sometimes it is from the conclusion of the argument, sometimes it is from a crucial or controversial premise which is key to that micro-argument. It is important, however, that in constructing the macro-argument one must pay close attention to representing the general sense of the entire passage. This is a tough task. What better way to accomplish this than by using the detailed micro-arguments at hand?

These chapter arguments, in turn, will be used in a similar way to construct book macro-arguments. In this way one can obtain exact understanding at a general level. This sort of comprehension is the most difficult to acquire. Often, people who pretend towards this mastery level are really full of vagueness and ambiguity. They find it hard to acquire the same rigor and precision that is more readily obtained at the micro level. And since much of a discipline's meaningful discourse takes place on the macro level, these critics are often in the position of not being able to clearly distinguish the good remarks from the bad: the appropriate wide-level generalizations from the callow and simplistic.

Macro-level outlining can go a long way to providing just such a standard and thus can be an appropriate tool for helping students control and understand the form of larger general-level discourse.

COMPARE AND CONTRAST

One example of the above can be found in the compare-and-contrast evaluation. As a rule, this sort of standard calls for the student to discover two complementary facets of a macro-argument. Thus, this type of evaluation can serve as an example of the use of macro-argumentation.

RULES

1. Find the appropriate body of text for each author called for in the compare-and-contrast evaluation.
2. Find the micro-outlines that cover the texts mentioned in rule 1.
3. Addressing one author at a time, create chapter- or other-level macro-outline(s) from the body of micro-outlines.
4. When macro-outlines are complete for both authors, compare the outlines side by side. Examine the types of conclusions each is trying to draw.
5. Make a list of associated tenets that attach to these conclusions. This list should be similar to the elemental analysis described in Table Eight of Chapter Seven.
6. Put each argument before you. Find the appropriate premises to evaluate according to the procedure described on p. 61 of Chapter Seven.
7. Decide what you feel to be right or wrong with each premise, using the procedures discussed in Chapter Eight—noting, where necessary, any logical fallacies (Chapter Nine).
8. Construct your essay from the viewpoint of the "correct" position (which may be a third alternative), using the authors involved as foils (much in the way that the counterarguments are used in the pro evaluation). The contrast and comparison points are thus to be made *only in so far* as such insights bear upon the "correct" position.

The two authors' premises and conclusions thus become springboards by which the correct view of things is revealed. Mere exposition of the authors (which is where many student essays of this type begin and end) is not sufficient to create an entire essay. Such exposition merely sets the stage for the real action to follow. As props and scenery they are there to enhance the drama—not to be the drama itself.

GENERAL QUESTIONS

The compare-and-contrast essay is one of many types of general questions. They are always most difficult for students to execute because they presuppose a rigorous limiting of the topic before beginning the essay.

Just because a question is broad in scope does not mean that a tight outline cannot be found to represent it. A good outline always suits the scope of the inquiry. The skill acquired through practice with micro-arguments is easily transferred to macro-arguments.

By completing one's skills at this second level of discourse, one has mastered the essential outlining technique. If this primer is being used in conjunction with various course readings, then this final step can be practiced by using the outlines already completed at the micro level. In my own teaching I often collect and examine several micro-arguments throughout the term and spend some time at the end of the course suggesting to the student ways to put his term's work together through creating various macro-level outlines.

Such a notebook of outlines, though time consuming to prepare, is invaluable to the student. It provides an in-depth appraisal of some particular text ready for instant review.

Learning how to prepare such rigorous reconstruction of a text allows the student to create an artifact of lasting value. Later, in business or some other profession, the same principles can be used to create hard-hitting reports and management presentations. The practical, applied value of this skill cannot be overemphasized.

For the reader who is not using this as part of another course of study, I would suggest taking some book or article that is of interest or of importance to your work and apply the outlining and evaluation techniques on the micro and macro levels.

FINAL REMARKS

We all want to confront the persuaders of this world with confidence. This modest volume proposes positive steps that can allow one to realize such an aspiration. If we are indeed best defined as thinking, rational animals, and if logic is the language of reason, then mastering the techniques of outlining and evaluation of logical argument is one of the most fundamental activities we can pursue. Competence in outlining and evaluation means that each of us may move one step closer to more fully realizing our humanity. And that's a goal well worth striving for.

READING QUESTIONS

1. What is the difference between a macro- and a micro-argument?
2. How can one analyze a macro-argument with precision?
3. What is the general strategy of compare-and-contrast questions?
4. How should one approach other types of general questions?

Answers

ANSWERS TO THE QUESTIONS ON PAGE 8

1. Speaker, audience, point of contention, argument, common body of knowledge.
2. Any example similar to that given on page 2 will do.
3. Any of the following:

    1. Measurements and standards of the circumstances.
        A. Setting up a measurement standard.
        B. Measuring by that standard.
    2. Making value judgments within the standard.
    3. Putting the standards into practice.

4. In the genetic order one begins with the conclusion and works to establish premises. These operate as cause and effect respectively. In the logical order the premises act as cause, and the conclusions function as effect.
5. They may persuade large groups more quickly and economically (though they do so illegitimately).
6. Through logical analysis. By establishing the crucial points one may acquire focus which allows one to pinpoint the source of error.

ANSWERS TO THE QUESTIONS ON PAGE 14

1. A topical outline gives a summary of all the key points within a passage.
2. A logical outline presents only the arguments within a passage. It carefully highlights premises and conclusions.
3. A logical outline describes the structure of arguments and nothing else. A topical outline provides information about classification not essential to the

argument and various side comments. Passages that are primarily persuasive should feature logical outline. Those which are not should feature topical outline.

4. Logical outlining demands a precise output. For this reason the student must have read the arguments very carefully and have an exact grasp of the subject matter. Comprehension is thus greatly increased.

5. The principle of fairness is: "Always reconstruct an argument in its strongest form even if it requires correcting trivial errors (though these may be noted elsewhere)." This is necessary in order to insure we are encountering the argument in its strongest form. It does little good to support or defeat a weak version since it may always be modified to become stronger.

ANSWERS TO THE QUESTIONS ON PAGES 23–24

EXERCISES ON CONTRADICTORY OPPOSITES

1. No
2. No
3. Yes
4. Yes
5. No

EXERCISES ON INDIRECT ARGUMENT

1. Thesis: One of the people in this house last night committed the murder—John, Mary, or Sally.
   This is an indirect argument by remainders. John and Sally could not have done it. Therefore, Mary did it.

2. Thesis: A completely flat tax of 20 percent should not be adopted.
   Antithesis assumed: A completely flat tax of 20 percent should be adopted.
   Antithesis leads to absurdity: A completely flat tax is unfair because it creates unequal tax burdens.
   Therefore, antithesis is wrong and thesis is proved.

READING QUESTIONS

1. A property of an argument in which all the premises are represented directly or indirectly in the conclusion.

2. A property of an inferential sentence. Read the premises cited as justifications. Then read the inferential sentence said to be supported by them. If one *must* accept the inferential sentence after agreeing to the supporting sentences, then the inference is "tight."

3. An argument is valid when it has interlocking premises and all its inferences are tight. An argument is sound when it is valid and all the premises are true.

4. Return to the text to see whether you've captured the intention of the text—including the additions of any extra premises.

5.   I.   Begin with the conclusion
    II.   Create a supporting argument
        A.   Listing and titling
        B.   Inferential combinations
        C.   Finalizing the argument
        D.   Assessing your argument

ANSWERS TO THE QUESTIONS ON PAGES 34–35

GROUP A

1. Inductive, enumeration.
2. Deductive.
3. Inductive, analogy.
4. Inductive, causation.
5. Deductive.

GROUP B

1. Inductive, agreement.
2. Inductive, joint method of agreement and difference.

ARGUMENTS ON COGENCY

1. Not cogent. Sample is incomplete.
2. Not cogent. No causal connection.
3. Cogent. Method of difference.
4. Not cogent (though close). Argument by analogy; however, the analogy is incorrect since by all accounts there is *no* completely satisfactory training for war.
5. Cogent. Method of agreement.

READING QUESTIONS

1. Enumerative induction lists all the observed properties of something with the objective of making a generalization about that type of thing. One draws a conclusion about all members of the class from premises that are about the observed members.
2. Analogy rests on the assumption that objects that are similar in certain respects will be similar in other respects as well.
3. Necessary conditions state that without the presence of some condition some specified effect will not occur. Sufficient conditions state that with the addition of some condition some specified effect will occur.
4. Method of agreement, method of difference, joint method of agreement and difference, and method of concomitant variation.
5. Deductive: valid inferences, true premises. Inductive: strong inferences, true premises.

ANSWERS TO THE QUESTIONS ON PAGE 45

EXERCISES (FROM P. 45)

1. The argument is:
   1. China is the largest country in the world.
   2. America can use all the allies it can get.
   3. America should cultivate China's friendship and support.

2. The argument is: 1. I am not a man whose nature it is to follow the crowd.
                        2. The other road is the road the crowd chooses.
                        3. It makes all the difference when you're true to your nature.
                        ___
                        4. The road less taken has made all the difference to me.

3. The argument is: 1. The NFL's rating system is a true indicator of a QB's relative talent.
                        2. Dan Marino is near the top of the NFL's QB rating system.
                        3. A QB's past performance will be continued in the future.
                        ___
                        4. Dan Marino will be one of the top QBs in NFL history.

4. The arguments are: 1. Murderers prey upon innocent civilians.
                        2. Terrorists prey upon innocent civilians.
                        ___
                        3. Terrorists are murderers.

                        1. Libya continues to support terrorists.
                        2. Whoever supports a group must take responsibility for their actions.
                        ___
                        3. Libya's leaders must share the responsibility for terrorists it supports.

Group B is left to the student
GROUP A EXERCISES (FROM PAGES 46–47)

1. [This argument is an enthymeme.]
2. [All people who made fascist broadcasts were imprisoned.]
3. [We should go to the game together.]
4. [You're not a member.]
5. [You're not a good driver.]
6. [Killing a fetus is wrong.]
7. [A fetus is merely a part of a woman's body.]

GROUP B

1. [One can only completely possess a definite, finite quantity.]
2. [Fred serves Mammon.]
3. [Orestes faces the torment of one not possessed of the divine union.]

ANSWERS TO THE QUESTIONS ON PAGES 48–56

Conclusions. (The following list is meant as an aid for those having trouble getting into the arguments for the purpose of outlining. I have listed only what I take to be the principal conclusion. There may be other subconclusions which should be inserted into the argument as an inference(s).)

CONTEMPORARY LIFE

1. (a) The trend of lower trash bag sales must change.
   (b) A.B.C.'s mighty trash bag is well worth buying.
2. Maryland is the place to vacation.
3. There are times when, in a community such as a university, differences should be set aside and the losing side accept the decision of the majority.
4. Informatics allows the small company to compete with the big one.
5. Political honor is a splendid torment.
6. Marriott has plenty of space for all one's convention needs.

HISTORY OF IDEAS

1. Tragedy is superior to epic poetry.
2. Liberty sometimes means finding help in obtaining the right direction of one's life.
3. (a) One cannot choose to be nothing.
   (b) One should always choose to exist.
   (c) Man cannot rightly choose not to exist.
4. I exist.
5. The immediate object of poetry is pleasure, and this pleasure comes from the whole.
6. Thesis: Piety is not defined as that which the gods love.
   Antithesis: Piety is defined as that which the gods love.

ANSWERS TO THE QUESTIONS ON PAGE 62

1. (a) Make clear the assessed character of that which is being evaluated (an argument, book, opera, movie, etc.); (b) analyze that character into its components; (c) direct attention to particular important components; (d) put forth a point of view directed through those components; (e) generate a reasoned argument for that point of view; and (f) show how one's view of the whole is affected by the positions taken on those components.
2. By creating a logical outline according to the procedures described in Chapter Two.
3. By first isolating the crucial premises and then by examining the most controversial of these.
4. A crucial premise is usually an assertion or a group of assertions. From among several candidates, the premise(s) which seem logically more fundamental will be taken to be crucial. Thus, from among three premises—A, B, and C—if B and C are shown to depend logically upon A, then A is more fundamental; therefore, more crucial.
5. A controversial premise is one which seems to have a greater number of disputable elements which are comprised within it.

ANSWERS TO THE QUESTIONS ON PAGE 68

1. (a) Create an outline and test it according to the method advocated in Chapter Two.

(b)   Decide which premises to evaluate (follow the procedure described in Chapter Seven and summarized on p. 61).

(c)   Decide what position you will take on this point(s). Your position will be either positive or negative. Depending on which you choose your evaluation will be either "pro" or "con." Whatever choice is made, the resulting viewpoint will be expressed through the premise(s) selected above.

(d)   Use the list created to judge the controversial premises to structure the resulting argument and essay.

2.   Con strategy: If the inferences of an argument are tight and the premises are interlocking, then the justification of the truth of the conclusion depends upon each one of the premises. Destroy one premise and you have undermined the conclusion.

3.   Pro strategy: You want to defend your author from the strongest attacks which could be made against the weakest or most controversial point. In this way you have helped the author where he needs it the most.

4.   Set out the elements of the points to be evaluated. Put down your responses according to whether you are writing a pro or a con essay.

Combine your responses and title them. Then use logical outlining to formalize your argument. Use this outline as the skeleton upon which you will construct your entire essay.

ANSWERS TO THE QUESTIONS ON PAGES 81–84

GROUP A

1.   Ad baculum
2.   Improper analogy
3.   Composition
4.   Amphiboly
5.   Equivocation
6.   Incomplete evidence
7.   Begging the question
8.   Changing the question
9.   Dilemma question
10.   Hasty generalization
11.   Division
12.   Incomplete evidence
13.   Equivocation
14.   Begging the question
15.   Changing the question
16.   Dilemma question
17.   Ad hominem
18.   Ignorance
19.   Pity
20.   Social identification
21.   Disconnected authority

22. Accent
23. Ignorance
24. Disconnected authority
25. Accent
26. Connected authority
27. False cause
28. Connected authority
29. False cause
30. Composition
31. Division
32. Improper analogy
33. Ad hominem

GROUP B

1. Equivocation and amphiboly.
2. Hasty generalization and improper analogy.
3. Argument against the speaker and improper analogy.
4. Changing the question.
5. Connected and disconnected authority.

ANSWERS TO THE QUESTIONS ON PAGE 93

1. A micro-argument takes place over a few paragraphs, up to several pages at most. Macro-arguments take place over an entire chapter or book. Micro-arguments are the building blocks for chapter macro-arguments. These, in turn, are used to construct book macro-arguments.
2. The same way one treats micro-arguments: with logical outlining. Since the space dimensions are expanded, extra care must be used in formulating the premises and point of contention.
3. Since this text advocates a critical approach to persuasion, only those parts of the authors' arguments which bear upon the "correct" view should be examined. "Correct" here is determined by the considered judgment of the reader. In this way "compare and contrast" is not a mere exercise in showing *what* each author said or believed, but instead advances a reasoned appraisal of the point in question.
4. The danger is responding in vague and imprecise terms which convey nothing of value. Rather, the student should use macro-argument outlines to give form to the question. Then, use macro-arguments to respond (using the same type of techniques described in micro-argument—the only difference is the level of generality). By providing form to the question, one goes a long way toward avoiding the dangers inherent to general questions.

Glossary

Accent. A fallacy of ambiguity in which multiple meanings are created due to the inclusion of the passage into an unusual context. (Chapter Nine)

Advertiser image. In pictorial argument the promotion of the institution itself, as opposed to any particular product from the institution. (Chapter Four)

Amphiboly. A fallacy of ambiguity in which two or more distinct meanings are created from a poorly formed grammatical structure. (Chapter Nine)

Analogy, Induction by. Analogy rests on the assumption that objects that are similar in certain respects will also be similar in other respects. (Chapter Three)

Appeal to pity. This fallacy persuades via an emotional appeal. (Chapter Nine)

Argument. An argument consists of at least two sentences, one of which purports logically to follow from the other. There are two large classes of argument: deductive and inductive. (Chapters Two and Three)

Argumentum ad baculum. See Argument from coercion.

Argumentum ad hominem. See Argument against the speaker.

Argument against the speaker. In this fallacy the argument itself is not attacked. Rather, one critiques the person putting forth the argument. This shifts the ground from where it should be. (Chapter Nine)

Argument from coercion. A fallacy that rests on the premise that might makes right. (Chapter Nine)

Argument from ignorance. This fallacy rests on the notion that a proposition is true simply because it has never been proven false, and vice versa. (Chapter Nine)

Assertion. The weakest justification. It means that the premise is true simply because one person has said it. The truth of the premise may be doubted. (Chapter Two)

Audience. The people at whom the argument is directed.

Authority, Argument from. This fallacy has two forms: connected and disconnected. In *disconnected* fallacy, an expert from one field reports on something about which he is not an expert. In *connected* fallacy, one accepts an expert's testimony on a subject which goes beyond the evidence and represents an analysis about something which is not agreed upon even by experts in that field. In this case the listener needs more than one expert's opinion. A logical argument is also required.

Begging the question. A fallacy in which one assumes what he is trying to prove. (Chapter Nine)

Causation, inductive argument. This type of inductive argument seeks to show that a set of antecedent conditions brings about a subsequent set of conditions via a scientifically recognized mechanism. (Chapter Three)

Chain argument (also called sorites).   A chain argument occurs when the conclusion of one argument becomes a premise in the subsequent argument.

Changing the question.   A fallacy in which one shifts the grounds of the argument from the issue under discussion to another issue for which an answer *is* readily available. (Chapter Nine)

Classification.   One of the three divisions of the text. This is a mode of analysis in which classes are created on the basis of a division made in the common body of knowledge. This can become a useful element for the argument (in which case it is included as a fact or assertion), or it can be of no direct importance to the argument (in which case it is included in a topical outline, but not in a logical outline). (Chapters One and Four)

Common body of knowledge.   One of the elements within the context of argument. It consists of a collection of facts and shared assumptions about what counts as a proper way to relate facts. (Introduction)

Compare and contrast.   A form of general evaluation in which a macro-argument provides the structure. The compare-and-contrast essay is a vehicle by which one may illustrate the "correct" position on a given point of contention. (Chapter Ten)

Composition, Fallacy of.   A false inference which states that properties properly assigned to the *part* may also be assigned to the *whole*. (Chapter Nine)

Conclusion.   This is what an argument aims for. The conclusion follows logically from the premises. Often, we call such sentences *conclusions* within the finished argument and *points of contention* apart from this environment. (Chapters Two and Three)

Context of argument.   The context of argument contains five elements which comprehensively describe the dynamics of logical persuasion: speaker, audience, point of contention, argument, and common body of knowledge. It may be adapted to pictorial argument as well. (Introduction and Chapter Four)

Contradictory opposites.   See Opposites.

Contrary opposites.   See Opposites.

Controversial premise.   A controversial premise is one which seems to have a greater number of disputable elements which are comprised within it. (Chapter Seven)

Crucial premise.   A crucial premise is usually an assertion or a group of assertions. Among several candidates the premise(s) which seems logically more fundamental will be taken to be crucial. Thus, from among three premises—A, B, C—if B and C are shown to depend logically upon A, then A is more fundamental, and therefore more crucial. (Chapter Seven)

Deductive argument.   An argument whose conclusion seeks to follow necessarily from the premises. (Chapters Two and Three)

Dilemma question.   This fallacy focuses attention away from the principal issue by offering false choices. (Chapter Nine)

Dividing the text.   The text may be divided into three parts: argument, classification, and side comments.

Division, Fallacy of.   A false inference which states that properties properly assigned to the *whole* may also be assigned to the *part*. (Chapter Nine)

Enumerative induction.   In enumerative induction the strategy is to list all the observed properties of something with the objective of making a generalization about that type of thing. (Chapter Three)

Equivocation.   A fallacy of ambiguity that operates by using one term and assigning two or more meanings to that term and then using whichever meaning suits the purpose— moving back and forth between meanings. (Chapter Nine)

Evaluation of an argument.   An evaluation is a reasoned response to a logical argument or to a fallacy. A "pro" response supports the author in question. A "con" evaluation seeks to disprove the author's contention. (Chapters Seven and Eight)

Fact.   This is the middle-strength justification. It means that most listeners would accept the given truth put forth as objectively correct. (Chapter Two)

Facts, Disputing of.   Facts may be disputed by developing one's examination of the following categories. (1) Measurements and standards of the circumstances: (a) setting up a measurement standard; (b) measuring by that standard. (2) Making value judgments within the standard. (3) Putting the standards into practice. (Introduction)

Fairness, Principle of.   Always reconstruct an argument in its strongest form even if it requires correcting trivial errors (though these may be noted elsewhere).

Fallacy of ambiguity. This is a classification of fallacy which contains three subclasses: equivocation, amphiboly, and accent. Ambiguity means that multiple meanings are created so that the author may refer to one at one moment and another at another; all to his advantage. (Chapter Nine)

False cause. A false inference which occurs when there is no good evidence by which to infer a causal relationship. (Chapter Nine)

False inference. A classification of fallacy which occurs when the inferences are drawn through improper exercise of the various rules of deduction and/or induction. There are three subclasses: false cause, composition, and division. (Chapter Nine)

Hasty generalization. This fallacy comes about when a broad conclusion is created from an atypical sample. (Chapter Nine)

Incomplete evidence. A fallacy in which one makes a judgment without having the salient portion of data available. This is because the evidence presented is not exhaustive. (Chapter Nine)

Indirect argument. This form of argument varies from direct argument because instead of having the point of contention proved positively, the logical complement is disproved or the possible choices are narrowed to one. (Chapter Two—Appendix)

Inference. This is formally the strongest justification. The inference is the vehicle which makes one accept some premise as a result of accepting other premises. The truth of the premise is thus dependent upon the truth of those other premises. (Chapters Two and Three)

Improper analogy. This fallacy occurs by incorrectly shifting the grounds of argument from properties belonging to one statement to those of another. Generally the former is well known and beyond dispute while the latter is controversial. There is no scientific mechanism to legislate this shift. (Chapter Nine)

Interlocking premises. A property of an argument which states that all the premises are represented directly or indirectly in the conclusion's inference. (Chapter Two)

Justification. A justification is the reason we accept a premise. In this book, the myriad of possible reasons have been simplified into three groups: assertion, fact, and inference. (Chapter Two)

Logical argument and reading comprehension. Higher than for a topical outline. This is because logical outlining requires exact, precise exposition of the mechanics of the argument. Such precise reconstruction requires a high level of understanding on the part of the reader. (Chapter One)

Logical complements. The argument assumes that if we want to prove a point (thesis), first assume its opposite (antithesis) and then show how that opposite leads us into an absurd (false) state of affairs.

Logical fallacy. A bad argument which does not persuade through logic. (Chapter Nine)

Logical outline. A logical outline presents only the arguments within a passage. It carefully highlights premises and conclusions. (Chapter One)

Loose inference. Whenever the relationship between a premise justified by "inference" and those listed to support it is such that this justification can be doubted, then the inference is loose. Used only in deductive arguments.

Macro-argument. The argument contained within larger sections of text—a chapter of a book. Though this section of text is of a grander scale, outlining can still be used to illumine the structure of the argument for more general evaluation.

Micro-argument. The argument found in short sections of text—anywhere from a few sentences to several pages. This scale of argument stands as the building block of larger macro-arguments.

Opposites. Contradictory opposites: Among two propositions which are contradictory opposites, these two propositions have opposite truth values. For example, if one is true, then the other must be false. (Chapter Two—Appendix). Contrary opposites: Among two propositions which are contrary opposites, one may not know for certain the truth value of one given any truth value for the other. (Chapter Two—Appendix)

Order of genesis. The order of genesis begins with the conclusion and works to establish premises. These operate as cause and effect respectively. (Introduction)

Order of logical presentation. In the logical order one begins with premises and works to the conclusion. These operate as cause and effect respectively. (Introduction)

Persuasion.   The act of trying to win another to your point of view. (Introduction and Chapter Nine)

Pictorial argument.   Persuasion which features a visual presentation. Like all argument it can be valid and sound (strong and cogent) or not. Often used in advertising.

Point of contention.   The exact statement about which you are trying to persuade another. Within a finished argument this is called the conclusion. (Introduction, Chapters Two and Three)

Premise.   The building block of an argument. Collectively the premises cause one to accept the conclusion.

Principle of fairness.   Always reconstruct an argument in its strongest form even if it requires correcting trivial errors (though these may be noted elsewhere).

Product image.   In pictorial argument, the promotion of the product itself. (Chapter Four)

Proposition.   A declarative sentence with truth value.

Reductio ad absurdum.   see Logical complements.

Remainders.   This principle of indirect argument assumes a limited number of cases. One can show one to be the case if the others are shown not to be the case. (Chapter Three)

Shifting the grounds.   A classification of logical fallacy that moves the focus of attention from the argument in question to something else (or uses something else to generate the conclusion). (Chapter Nine)

Shifting the terms.   A class of logical fallacy in which inferences are invalid because the terms themselves have been altered in some way. (Chapter Nine)

Side comments.   One of the three divisions of the text. Anything which is not an argument or a classification will be labeled a side comment. This information is more pertinent to a topical outline than to a logical outline.

Social identification.   This fallacy relies upon social pressure and a "me, too" principle. It suggests that popular acceptance can be equated with logical correctness. (Chapter Nine)

Sound argument.   An argument is sound if it is valid and all the premises are true. When an argument is sound we must accept the conclusion.

Sorites.   See Chain argument.

Speaker.   The person putting forth the argument.

Suppressed premise.   These are premises that are needed to make an inference but are not explicitly made by the writer. (Chapter Five)

Thematic context.   Useful in determining what is a premise and a conclusion. By noting the point of the passage, the conclusion should become clear. The premises are the material used to support the conclusion. (Chapter Five)

Tight inference.   Whenever the relationship between a premise justified by "inference" and those listed to support it is such that this justification cannot be doubted, then the inference is tight. Used only in deductive arguments.

Topical outline.   A topical outline gives a summary of all the key points within a passage. (Chapter One)

Valid argument.   A deductive argument is valid when all the inferences are tight and all the premises interlocking. In a valid argument, if one were to accept all the premises, he would have to accept the conclusion.

Word clues.   Certain words which also aid one in determining what is a premise or conclusion. (Chapter Five)

Index